Communing with

JESUS'
REAL PRESENCE

"Father Herbert Smith shares with us the ardor of his own spirit. Each chapter begins with a reflection on Jesus that is drawn deeply from the Christian tradition and expressed in fresh images. Then he turns the tradition into prayer that enables the reader to approach the sacred moment of Communion with a new appreciation of the great Gift of His Presence."

Thomas M. King, S.J.
Department of Theology
Georgetown University
Washington, D.C.

———— ✍ ————

"*Communing with Jesus' Real Presence* is a reflection of a priest's deep eucharistic faith. The subtitle holds the key to approaching the book. You don't read it. You meditate with him, line by line, in the time-honored tradition of Saint Ignatius' Second Method of Prayer—pausing whenever a passage strikes you and invites you to let the Holy Spirit take over."

Mark Link, S.J.
Author *(Vision, Mission, Action)*

Communing with
JESUS'
REAL PRESENCE

Holy Communion Meditations
and Eucharistic Adoration

Herbert F. Smith, S.J.

Christian Classics™

Allen, Texas

Nihil Obstat
Rev. Andrew J. Golias
Censor Librorum
November 15, 1996

Imprimatur
Most Rev. Anthony Cardinal Bevilacqua
Archbishop of Philadelphia
November 18, 1996

Imprimi Potest
Rev. James R. Stormes, S.J.
Provincial of the Maryland Province
December 2, 1996

Acknowledgments

The Scripture quotations contained herein are from the *New Revised Standard Version Bible: Catholic Edition,* copyright © 1993 and 1989 by the Division of Christian Education for the National Council of the Churches of Christ in the U.S.A. Used by permission. All rights reserved.

Send all inquiries to:
Christian Classics
An RCL Company
200 East Bethany Drive
Allen, Texas 75002-3804

Telephone: 800-264-0368 / 972-390-6400
Fax: 800-688-8356 / 972-390-6560

E-mail: cservice@rcl-enterprises.com

Website: **www.ThomasMore.com**

Printed in the United States of America

Library of Congress Catalog Number: 2003102136

6847   ISBN 87061-230-1

1 2 3 4 5   07 06 05 04 03

"Although you have not seen him, you love him;
and even though you do not see him now,
you believe in him and rejoice
with an indescribable and glorious joy,
for you are receiving the outcome of your faith,
the salvation of your souls"
(1 Peter 1:8–9).

OUR SAVIOR PRAYER

Our Savior from the Father's side,
Lord of all the world,
Save us by your side and heart once pierced,
Save us by your death and rising.
Call us, Shepherd Jesus,
To follow you and find salvation.
Lead us to the pasture of life's food,
And gather us into one flock
In your own sheepfold.
Guard us from the foe,
And guide us to our Father's home.

CONTENTS

Preface

WHY BELIEVE the Eucharist is what Jesus said it is? People at Capernaum asked Jesus for evidence to support the faith in the Eucharist to which he called, and he gave it. Unlike those people, we believe Jesus' teaching about the Eucharist because of our faith in him as Son of God. We believe in the Real Presence not by a leap in the dark, but on the authority of Jesus as God revealing. But there is no reason not to confirm our faith by the evidence, which he gave on that day in Capernaum, for believing the Eucharist is what he said it is. And so we consider that evidence now.

What I am referring to is the day at Capernaum that Jesus first spoke of the Eucharist. Here, in boiled-down form from the sixth chapter of Saint John, is the exchange that day between Jesus and his challengers:

THE PEOPLE: What are the works of God we're to do?

JESUS: Believe in the One the Father sent.

THE PEOPLE: Why should we believe in you? So you multiplied bread once. Through Moses it was done for forty years. What sign, what work can you do?

JESUS: I am the true bread from heaven. I am the bread of life; whoever comes to me will never hunger, and whoever believes in me will never thirst.

There! That is the reason Jesus himself gave why they should believe that the Eucharist is what Jesus said it is: *Experience! The Eucharist proves itself!* Those who eat his body and drink his blood will never hunger or thirst again.

We must understand this promise in the sense Jesus meant it. He had just warned people not to put their hearts into laboring for perishable bread. Clearly, he is talking about the hunger and thirst of the human heart. The human heart hungers for life to the full, and thirsts for the fullness of love. Jesus is claiming that the Eucharist fills both hungers.

Some Catholics are living proof that *they* experience what he promised. They would rather miss their three meals a day than their daily Holy Communion. They would sooner risk their lives than risk losing the Mass and the bread of life. Saint Francis de Sales is an example. Saint Leonard of Port Maurice recounts how Francis risked his life in the winter of 1596. He had to cross a bridge to get to the church. The bridge, partly washed out by rising waters, had an icy plank laid across the missing section. Despite his friends' pleading not to, he crept over the slippery plank daily on hands and knees so as not to miss his Mass and his Eucharist.

When Saint Therese of the Child Jesus used to drag herself from her sick bed to get to Mass daily, another Sister cautioned her against such exertion. She answered, "Oh, what are these sufferings to me in comparison with one Holy Communion?"

In churches around the land, you will find ordinary-looking people attending Mass daily, in rain or snow, sunshine or bitter cold. But they are not ordinary in this, they have experienced what Jesus called us to experience in the Eucharist. There must be days when they don't feel well, when they don't feel like stirring from bed or home, yet they come. They come because bodily hunger for comfort is endured to satisfy their hunger and thirst for life and love.

Some years ago during the post-Vatican II change and unrest in the Church, a national news weekly did an article on the Mass. This reader sensed in the article a hardly-suppressed amazement that so many Catholics continued faithfully to attend Sunday Mass. These Catholics, too, were finding at least a taste of what Jesus said we would find in the Eucharist.

Those who don't experience what Jesus promised should try to uncover the obstacles preventing it. Just as bodily food fails to produce some of its good effects in sick or indisposed people, spiritual food does not produce some of its good effects if the spirit is sick.

A parable will make the point clearer. A man had a young friend with a crippled leg. He learned from his friend all he could about the condition of his leg, then consulted an osteopath. The doctor was reasonably sure he could restore the leg, but would have to examine the patient to be certain. When the man told his crippled friend the good news, the cripple showed no interest. After some probing, the reason became evident. The crippled young man had become used to living on his disability check. He was in dread of facing a future without a guaranteed income.

If we are enslaved and clinging to the "benefits" of some sin in our lives, the life and love that Christ promises us through the Eucharist will find no ready response in us.

These meditations can help us stir a return of love to the Heart of Jesus. They draw us into the full range of the eucharistic mystery. There is no Eucharist without the Holy Sacrifice. Only by offering Mass can the priest consecrate the bread of heaven, which the Father shares with us. "The Eucharist is above all else a sacrifice" (Pope John Paul II, *Dominicae Cenae,* 9). When Jesus gave us the Eucharist at the Last Supper, he said, "This cup that is poured out for you is the new covenant in my blood" (Luke 22:20). That is to say, it is the fullness of his love for us, sealed by his redemptive offering on Calvary.

This brings up a final point. What we are meant to find in the Eucharist is not mere feelings of devotion but God himself. Saint Thomas Aquinas writes that the act of faith reaches out not just to a statement about God but to God himself. Similarly, our act of faith in the Real Presence ends not in words of belief about the Real Presence but in embracing the Real Presence. It ends not in a statement but in an experience.

It is this possession of God in the flesh that wins our hearts. And through this possession we begin beforehand to taste the resurrection and eternal life. This is what quenches our spiritual hunger and thirst far more than sweet consolations. Still, there should be such consolations too. Theologians tell us that, in a way parallel to natural food, eating the bread of life is meant to awaken pleasure, restore our strength, and nurture growth.

When we are full of loving feelings for God, they are his gift to us. But when, with feelings lacking, we persist in daily Mass and Communion because our hearts are finding life and love despite the absence of feelings, this is our gift of self to him. In both cases, we experience what he promised, the end of that disordered hunger and thirst which drives worldly people to fill an ocean of desire by spoonfuls of worldly pleasures and possessions. So we begin our meditations confident that we will find in the Eucharist what Jesus promised, the end of the hunger and thirst which God put in us to be filled only by the Incarnation and the Eucharist.

We bolster this confidence with the conviction of the Church that the Eucharist is rich beyond measure: "The other sacraments, as well as every ministry of the Church and every work of the apostolate, are linked with the Holy Eucharist and are directed toward it. For the most blessed Eucharist contains the Church's entire spiritual wealth, that is, Christ himself, our Passover and living bread. Through his very flesh, made vital and vitalizing by the Holy Spirit, he offers life to men. They are thereby invited and led to offer themselves, their labors, and all created things together with him" (Vatican II, *Decree on the Life and Ministry of Priests*).

Herbert F. Smith, S.J.

PART ONE

All About
Jesus and Us

INTRODUCTION

THE WHEAT ROSE FROM THE HILLSIDE on supple stalk and the ripe ears merged into a sea of burnished amber that flowed in golden waves whenever the late summer winds stirred restlessly. This was the perennial growth of living bread, which we call the "staff of life." Living now, it would die to become bread to nourish human bodies. The wheat would not give people life; they would give it life. After it had died and been eaten, they would transform it into their own life and flesh.

This is not the story of that lifeless bread. This is an account of the living bread which does not receive life from our bodies, but gives life to our souls and our bodies. This bread is not something but Someone. It is bread not from nature but from God. "I am the living bread that came down from heaven. Whoever eats of this bread will live forever" (John 6:51).

This heavenly bread, too, died that it might become our food. "Very truly, I tell you, unless a grain of wheat falls into the earth and dies, it remains just a single grain; but if it dies, it bears much fruit" (John 12:24). One grain of wheat, planted in the ground to die, springs up into a whole stalk, rich with many grains. The body of Jesus was laid in the ground for three days and rose as the center of a whole mystical body throbbing with his life. The natural grain of wheat dies twice; first, when it falls into the ground; second, when it is crushed into wheat. Jesus died once, pierced upon the cross. He sprang up on Easter morn, the sweet bread of eternal life, which disperses the black night of death as the morning sun laughs away the fears of night. "Where, O death, is your victory? Where, O death, is your sting?" (1 Corinthians 15:55). As the heliotrope turns ever toward the sun, the true lovers of life turn to Jesus, the Living Bread.

What prepares one to sit at the banquet table of this celestial Bread? Only the rebirth through baptism that makes us conscious of living a new life as a child of God. Grafted into the life of Christ, we need to be nourished by the bread of heaven and "drink with joy from the Savior's fountains." This life calls for union, in the Prince of Sacraments, with the divine Bridegroom the Father has presented to our souls.

But not once only is the joy of this union given to God's children. The bread which is Jesus is our daily bread, if our spiritual appetite is great enough to overcome all the barriers to the daily banquet. There is need, then, not only for baptism, but for daily growth, that we may be drawn to the chalice of our inebriation day by day. The best preparation for receiving Jesus tomorrow is to receive him today. Another great help is a day full of charity and service to his mystical body. Prayer and longing for Jesus complement these two activities. Meditation and spiritual reading crown them. Thus is the longing of our souls awakened.

1

JESUS

THE BEGINNING OF TRUE HOLINESS is to look on
Jesus. John the apostle never forgot that day of his youth
when his eyes first rested on the Son of Man. There along the
banks of the Jordan, John found passing before him the living
mystery of humanity united with divinity. How perfect that
union was he would not then have dared to guess.

A virgin had conceived and her son walked along the
water's edge in the spring sun as he watched. Mary, "tainted
nature's solitary boast," as William Wordsworth described her,
had flowered and the flower was here. In Jesus, humanity and
divinity had met. In Jesus, human and divine had kissed the
everlasting kiss of peace. The only son of a virgin, the only
Son of God, was walking the banks of the Jordan that
morning.

John did not know all this at that time but he did find
before him the mystery of a man marked with the divine. He
could not but look with approval upon the man, gracious and
strong, passing tranquilly along the Jordan's shore. And he
heard ringing in his ears the strange words of John the
Baptizer who pointed to Jesus. John had heard the Baptizer

preach often before, since he was his disciple, but never had the Baptizer spoken in tones like these. Wonder, gladness, finality rang across the morning air, like a bell pealing at last the end of a terrible night. "Here is the Lamb of God who takes away the sin of the world!" (John 1:29). And then, like the bell whose echoes slowly diminish, never to be heard again, or like the stars which fade from view when the light of day shines strong, the Baptizer faded from John the apostle's gaze and he saw "no one except Jesus himself alone" (Matthew 17:8).

 ## Prayer

"Sir, we wish to see Jesus!" (John 12:21).

My divine Savior, I make my own these words of the Greek people who pleaded with Philip to be taken to you.

May my desire to see you be as much greater than theirs as my knowledge of you exceeds theirs.

They hoped you would lead them to holiness, Jesus; I know you are my holiness.

They knew you must be a prophet from God; I know you are the Son of God.

They had hope that you would help them; I know you have loved me and died bleeding on the cross for me.

Divine Jesus, if I cannot yet have the great joy of gazing on you with my human eyes, I believe that I am about to receive a far greater gift.

For however great the joy of seeing you, far greater is the joy of giving myself to you and receiving you personally into my heart and soul.

Nothing suffices except that I be as closely united with you as Mary in the days when she carried you within her.

The sensible joy of seeing you would be great indeed; yet I would not trade that for my Christian birthright of Holy Communion.

In this sacrament I do not merely behold you, Jesus; in this sacrament there is no longer you and I, Jesus.

After this beloved communion there is "no one, but only Jesus." I no longer live, but it is you who live in me.

2

THE MYSTERY OF JESUS

THE MORE we know Jesus, the greater is the mystery of Jesus. Learning of Jesus is like plunging into the mysterious depths of the ocean. Only as we go down and down do we begin to experience the interminable expanses on every side. In like manner, until the implications of the mystery that is Jesus begin to break in on us, like waves from an unknown sea, we have hardly begun to know Jesus. At night, when the sky is overcast, we are surrounded by the unknown of the dark earth. But when the sky at last clears, we look up and are engulfed in the greater mystery of the whole universe.

Think of Mary, and the waves of mystery that rolled in upon her life from the day the angel first spoke the name of Jesus. Consider the insoluble mystery of God's seeming abandonment of her and his beloved, her son. The first time she saw her little son, it was in the cold poverty of a stable; the last time she saw him in his mortal life, he was dying terribly and shamefully on a cross. To this day, all this is a scandal to the nonbeliever. Nor was it clear to Mary. "Child, why have you treated us like this?" (Luke 2:48).

Strangers came into her life and told her things about Jesus and herself, which she, his mother, the chosen woman, did not know. Shepherds and wise men from the East made her ponder in her heart. Simeon walked into her life, took her child from her, and pronounced strange prophesies woven of celestial light and Stygian darkness and a sword that must pierce her heart.

The person of Jesus is the wonderful focus of all these deep mysteries. He is a man but not a human person. He is a divine Person, but with a human nature. He has a human soul resonant to all that is significant to human beings; and united with the affections of that soul beats his human heart, responsive to all that is worthy of human love. Yet within that same person is the infinity, the very being, of the eternal Son of God, to which that human body and soul are united. In him, in his eternal existence, this body and soul of his has its reality, and had its beginning on the day "the Word became flesh and lived among us" (John 1:14).

"No one has ever seen God," the Gospel of John tells us (1:18). Only after Jesus had died and risen was the way to glory opened. Only then did the vision of the ineffable God burst in all its glory upon the just who had died in the Lord. We who think we know Jesus have not even seen him in the flesh; we are as yet incapable of beholding him in the unspeakable radiance of his divinity. And still beyond this is the mystery of his eternal coming forth as Son of the Father: "You are my son; today I have begotten you" (Psalm 2:7). And still further is the mystery of the Holy Spirit, the Person of Love issuing from the Father and the Son. And still beyond is the final mystery of all, the great mystery of love in which the three divine Persons live and abide within one another in the mystery of the one God.

All of this is the mystery of Jesus, Son of Mary and the Father. For Jesus is God.

 ## Prayer

O Jesus, what you once said to your apostle, Philip, you can also say to me: "Have I been with you all this time, Philip, and you still do not know me?" (John 14:9).

Jesus, if I could look into your divine eyes and behold the mysteries there, I might understand.

Jesus, at the Last Supper, John rested his head upon your breast and learned the mysteries of your heart.

After that he had a new name for himself: the disciple whom Jesus loved.

After that he knew you, and he wrote, "God is love" (1 John 4:8).

And legend says of him that in his old age his one simple message to everyone was, "Little children, love one another."

Jesus, it is only with some understanding of who you really are that I can come to you in Holy Communion without sham and without pretense.

Jesus, alongside your love, mine is as a little candle flickering in the winds of temptation, shaded by your hand.

You are the Beginning and Eternity.

In your presence I am too small even to make the fuss of impressive comparisons.

Jesus, in Holy Communion this day, I want to be with you quietly, unobtrusively, hidden in a corner of your heart, communing wordlessly with you, trusting in you, and knowing that you are my God.

3

SPEAKING THE
NAME OF JESUS

IT IS A WONDERFUL EXPERIENCE to hear the person completely in love with Jesus speak the name of Jesus. Spoken however softly, the name stands out among other words as the bright silver moon dominates the starlit night. The name of Jesus appears on the horizon of sound with calm, majestic, mysterious beauty, like an Oriental ship gliding up from the East, lying low on the waters with cargo of jade and gold, frankincense and myrrh. Adoration is in the word, and hint of ineffable vision, and love so deep and so vast that the one single word says: "My love for Jesus cannot be contained by me or by my words any more than spring can be contained by one green blade, or fall by one golden leaf fluttering to earth in the sun. I am a part of all who love Jesus and all who love him are part of me. Alone, I cannot support my love."

Yet true love is not content with breathing the name of Jesus, for deeds speak with more certain tongue. The lover of Jesus engraves the record of his love deep into all the moments of his life. Does the writer speak in words, the artist in oils, the sculptor in stone? The lover of Jesus speaks in actions that carve his whole life and substance into an exquisite image of Jesus—a living, breathing image of Jesus. This is the way Jesus should be spoken. This is why he is called the Word, that is, One who comes forth spiritually from another. The Word of the Father he is, from all eternity; the flesh-clad Word of Mary from the day of his birth in Bethlehem; now the Word incarnated in the bodies and souls of all who speak in deeds the beloved name of Jesus, to make themselves his perfect members.

The name of Jesus that leaps from the lips is lovely. The deeds of Jesus that issue from our devotion to him are lovelier. Most radiantly beautiful of all is the act by which body and soul are given to Jesus to be one with him. We "speak" Jesus with our very substance when we offer ourselves completely to him in the divine union of sacramental Communion.

Prayer

Divine Jesus, it is joy for me to hear your name spoken and to form its blessed sounds upon my own lips.

In this one word is summed up our hopes and our salvation.

Only those whom the Father teaches can speak with understanding this name hidden from the foundation of the world.

May your Father teach me, Jesus, to understand. I ask it of him in your name.

I ask that not my lips alone but my heart and mind and flesh may express your name by living your life, Jesus.

May I so live your life, Jesus, that even before I am united to you in Holy Communion I can say: "I live; now not I, but Jesus lives in me!"

And if this be so before Communion, what shall I say of Communion itself?

Words from my lips can say nothing of it, Jesus.

The Word of our living Communion alone can express what is so near to divinity.

Come swiftly, Jesus!

4

GIVING SELF TO JESUS

NO ONE CAN GIVE what he does not possess. A king who surrenders his kingdom to conquering enemies can bequeath to his son nothing but an empty title.

We, too, if we would give ourselves to Jesus, must first possess ourselves. We are incapable of giving Jesus a pure heart if our heart still belongs to any sin at all. Nor can we give him a generous heart if our heart is steeped in self. If our eyes and ears and hands still yield to sinful pleasures, they are slaves of sin and not in our power to give.

We must employ all the weapons in the arsenal of grace to win the spiritual freedom by which alone we truly possess ourselves. Only when, by good use of the graces Jesus won for us, we too win the victory, can we present ourselves as pure and holy gifts to Jesus. Only in the triumph of this conquest do we ascend with Jesus from the altar of Calvary, a victim offered in the odor of sweetness to God the Father. To live without sin is to do God's will. And doing his will is the only acceptable sacrifice.

This battle for sinlessness is not fought and won overnight. Our bodies and souls are vast countries suffering betrayal from within and enemy onslaughts from without. The attacks will not cease until Satan has wrested every last vestige of freedom and self-possession from us; or until, resisting to the end, we pass through the portals of death from which Christ has stripped away the gargoyles of terror. We must arm courageously against the fifth column of our passions and bad habits plaguing us from within. We must resist the enticements of the world, false friends, and the devil, whether their attack be by subversion or by open assault. It is no easy thing to ward off corruption and enslavement of the body and soul, which we long to purify, free, and offer to God.

Victory, however, is sweet, and not only worth every effort, but beyond all price. In the gloriously risen and triumphant Jesus of Holy Communion, we have the model and goal that we must set ourselves, looking to the day when we too shall rise spotless and immortal. In Jesus we have the divine Beloved to whom we want to come daily in full self-possession so that we may give ourselves altogether to him, and forever be fully his possession.

 ## Prayer

In the shadow of the cross, Jesus, your radiant body came forth like sunrise from a now-empty tomb.

You stood, a lone Man upon a hill, graceful and quiet in the nobility of your conquest, surveying with quiet joy the scene of your victory.

In you, Jesus, the race of Adam and Eve had conquered sin, had fought with death and won!

Jesus, my Savior and my God, this very day in Holy Communion you come to me radiant and fresh from your eternal triumph.

You step out of eternity into my heart, just as you stepped into eternity a moment ago from your risen tomb.

The victory is forever yours, Jesus!

Not for yourself alone did you win this victory, Jesus.

The eternal life that burned in you like a holy flame when you rose from the dead is my life too.

"Those who eat my flesh and drink my blood have eternal life," you told us, "and I will raise them up on the last day" (John 6:54).

When today you come to me in your divinity, your soul, your body, and your blood, deepen in me your life, beloved Jesus.

May the fountain of your strength and your holiness well up in me to help me win complete victory over self and sin in these days of my mortal life.

Give me the will for this hard fight, Jesus, and the generosity to give myself as completely to you as you have given yourself to me.

And on the day of my resurrection, when the fountain of your youth wells up in me to produce everlasting life, how glad I will be that I have won a complete victory!

How glad I will be that I fought with the sword of grace to win self-mastery that I might be given completely to you.

I promise you, I will live for that day, beloved Jesus.

5

BROTHERS AND SISTERS OF CHRIST

THERE ARE MANY BANDS of brothers and sisters, but true Christians are members of the happiest band of all. Our brother is the natural, only-begotten Son of God. To Jesus himself, this fellowship with us is a great treasure, for he rejoiced "in his inhabited world and delight[ed] in the human race" (Proverbs 8:31). He often referred to himself as the Son of Man, and after he arose he directed Mary Magdalene to carry to his brethren the message, "I am ascending to my Father and your Father, to my God and your God" (John 20:17).

By his conception and birth from a human mother, Jesus became our brother. We became his brothers and sisters when his divine Father became our own through the sacrament of rebirth. "Very truly, I tell you, no one can enter the kingdom of God without being born of water and Spirit" (John 3:5). Baptism alone gives us membership in this happiest of fraternal bands. Jesus was baptized before us, says Saint Gregory Nazianzen, "to bury sinful humanity in the waters, and to sanctify the Jordan for our sake and in readiness for us." The sun has since evaporated those waters and distributed them round the world to sanctify the waters that gave us baptism.

To be a child is not yet to be a grownup. Many vicissitudes lie, like snares, along the path of growth. In like manner, to be born into divine life is not yet to enjoy the stature of full-grown children of God. The nourishment of our supernatural life must come immediately from God, day by day. Yet there is also much for us to do. The laws of spiritual growth are similar to those governing the maturing process of the natural body. Daily exercises in the service of God are needed to bring us to the fullness of spiritual manhood or womanhood. Once when Jesus was told that his Mother and brothers were nearby he said, "For whoever does the will of my Father in heaven is my brother and sister and mother" (Matthew 12:50). By diligent effort to learn God's will, and by carrying it out at any cost, we will win for ourselves everlasting fellowship among this happiest band of brothers and sisters.

 Prayer

Eternal and everlasting Son of God, it is through your graceful descent to earth, through your donning of our human nature, that I have come to know and love better what it means to be a human being.

All the lowliness and humiliations of our nature, so far below the mighty angels, are easily borne, now that you are one of us.

In fact, it is now we who are to be envied, because we have for true and natural brother God's dear and only-begotten Son.

My divine Savior, can anyone sum up what you are to us and mean to us?

Saint Columban the Abbot said that "you are our all: our life, our light, our salvation, our food and our drink, our God."

And we, in turn, what are we, what can we be to you?

You yourself told us that when we do the will of your heavenly Father, we can be brother and sister and mother to you—as if to say we will then be all that we can be for you.

Then come into my heart in Holy Communion this morning, Jesus, and make me mysteriously "brother and sister and mother" to you according to the desire of your own heart.

Help me to live my life in your image.

You begged the Father to make us one in you, Jesus, and now I beg him for the same favor.

I know that this union begins in mind and will, so that we think the same way and love the same things and carry out what thought and love say must be done.

By your grace and favor I can become a radiant image of your human love and service of the Father.

Give us the gifts we need, divine Brother, to be truly your brothers and sisters.

6

--- ～ ---

TRUE BROTHERS AND SISTERS

NONE BUT SONS AND DAUGHTERS who share one father and have the same mother are full and true brothers and sisters. The love that they share for the selfsame mother, who nourished them at her breast and guided them as they toddled along at her knee, enriches and cements their love for one another. In like manner, love and imitation of the same strong father conforms them to his image and further deepens their mutual respect and affection.

All of us who have been born of water and the Holy Spirit have God for our Father. By living in the image of Jesus, our model, we grow in the likeness of our divine Father. But we cannot be like Jesus unless his loves are also our loves. And the deepest love of Jesus, after his burning love for his God and Father, is his most tender, devoted love for his Virgin Mother, Mary. To be like Jesus, we must not only have Mary for our mother but we must know her and love her with all our heart, as does Jesus.

The deeper our love for Mary, the more we will sense the supernatural truth that Jesus is our brother, and the more fully our hearts will find themselves opening to the love and the gifts of love Jesus our brother offers us. This mystery of love is prefigured in Joseph, one of the twelve sons of Jacob. Joseph, who saved his whole family from death by starvation, is a figure of Jesus, Savior of all his human family.

Joseph loved all his brothers, even after they sold him into slavery out of jealousy. But he cherished most his beloved youngest brother, Benjamin, who was not a half-brother like the rest but was son of his beautiful mother, Rachel. In fact, beautiful Rachel sacrificed her life in giving birth to Benjamin. When Joseph's brothers came into Egypt to seek food and met him there, he longed most of all to see Benjamin. It is no wonder then that Scripture recounts for us how, when Joseph at last beheld Benjamin once again, his heart went out to his youngest brother, and he was so moved he cried.

When we wait at the banquet table of Holy Communion for food and salvation from our divine Brother Jesus, he longs most of all to find there his very own brother and sister, child of God and of his beautiful Virgin Mother, Mary, whom he gave to all of us on Calvary when he said, "Here is your Mother" (John 19:27). Who can fathom the love in the heart of this divine Brother when his gaze rests upon a brother or sister who recognizes and cherishes Mary for their mutual Virgin Mother? Will his Heart be less moved than was Joseph's heart for his brother Benjamin?

 ## Prayer

I pray with all my heart, Lord, that when you find me waiting and longing to receive you, you will always find in me one born of your own divine Father and human Mother by the mystery of grace.

Jesus, I pray for a most tender, most faithful, most holy love of our Mother.

You brought forth the mystical body from your wounded side during your sleep on Calvary, as Adam's spouse was taken from his side while he lay asleep in the Garden of Eden.

Mary was there, Jesus, and died the mystical death of sorrow when she held your pierced body in her arms after you had expired.

She, who knew only joy at your birth, felt the sword of sorrow pierce her heart when your mystical body was delivered.

Our Mother died a thousand deaths when I was born, my divine Brother.

Love me for all the sorrows she was willing to endure to give me to you.

My mother Mary, I love you.

I am grateful to you for bringing forth my Savior.

I am most grateful for having you as my mother in the mystical body of Jesus.

Adorn my heart and soul, Mary, with the qualities that will make Jesus recognize me, when he comes in Holy Communion this day, as a child of his own beloved Mother.

Be pleased to grant my request, most gracious Virgin and Mother, Mary.

7

---- ✒ ----

ONE ONLY JESUS

THERE IS ONLY ONE JESUS. Do you speak of the eternally begotten in the bosom of the Father? It is Jesus. Do you speak of the baby boy crying in the cold air of Bethlehem? "[Y]ou will name him Jesus" (Luke 1:31). Do you point to me, to yourself, to the black man, the yellow man, the poor man, the rich man? You are pointing to Jesus in his members. "[Y]ou are the body of Christ," says Saint Paul, "and individually members of it" (1 Corinthians 12:27). This truth was branded forever into Paul's consciousness on the day he fell blinded to the ground crying, "Who are you, Lord?" and heard the answer, "I am Jesus, whom you are persecuting" (Acts 9:5). In persecuting Christians, Paul was striking at Jesus, a man whom he knew was crucified and thought was dead.

The divine Bridegroom, the second Adam, bowed his sacred head and fell asleep upon the cross. During that sleep of death, the soldier opened his most sacred side all the way to his heart. From his side and from his heart the Father drew forth his mystical bride, the Church. The reason the Father let his second Adam sleep the sleep of death is to draw us forth from his side in order to present us to him when he awoke into his life on Easter morn.

Mary is my mother because I am a member of her only son. Every Christian is my brother or sister because we are children of the same Mother; because in living the life of Jesus, we have the same Father, God; and because we have the one, same brother, Jesus, our life!

It is in Jesus, our life, that we are more than brothers. "I am the vine, you are the branches," Jesus discloses to us (John 15:5a). Vine and branches are not many things; they are one thing. Legs, arms, head, are but one thing, the body. I dare not strike you, unless I am willing to strike Jesus. You dare not despise another's color, or turn cold eyes on the poor man, unless you want to despise Jesus, or look with cold eyes on Jesus hungry, Jesus naked, Jesus lonely and sick. "You that are accursed, depart from me into the eternal fire prepared for the devil and his angels; for I was hungry and you gave me no food . . ." (Matthew 25:41–42). Jesus encompasses us about on every side. There is only one Jesus and we must learn to recognize him. It is not easy. "He came to what was his own, and his own people did not accept him" (John 1:11). The eyes of love alone recognize the one only Jesus.

 ## Prayer

Jesus, it is even harder to recognize you in your brethren than to find you in the piece of bread the priest breaks!

At least the host is pure and white, good and wholesome, and can stand as a symbol of your pure, good, life-giving self.

With a simple, trusting act of faith, Jesus, I accept your word, in which you promise to be my food and my life present under the form of bread.

But how much harder, Jesus, it is to find your holy presence in sin and corruption of every kind!

In people holier, more noble, more blessed than myself, I can sometimes find you easily.

But in the indifferent, the selfish, the cruel, it is hard to find you, Jesus.

Yet, however hard, I must find you in them.

Would I have found you in the beaten bloody criminal hanging disgraced on a cross one Friday afternoon, mocked by law and order and passersby alike?

Would I have passed on in disgust or indifference that day, my God?

Might I not have disdained you, since those mocking you would have told me what a sinner and blasphemer you were?

Divine Jesus, make me like your saints, who kissed and cared for the most revolting of human beings for your sake.

Divine Jesus, make me like you, who touched lepers to help them and sat down with us sinners to heal us and who died for us because you loved us, and even became our brother.

Jesus, I will accept your word of command and find you in all your mystical body so that I can find you with all love in Holy Communion.

8

JESUS LOVING

THE BURNING LOVE in the Heart of Jesus when he comes to his least member in Holy Communion is a mystery beyond all appreciation and understanding. This does not mean that we should not try to understand; it means we should try the harder, for the love of Jesus is our greatest treasure and even the faintest appreciation of the Eucharist is a joy.

This love of Jesus for us involves three great mysteries. First is the mystery of the divine person of Jesus, who loved us before we were even created, and who now loves us with a human soul and a heart of flesh just like our own. The second mystery involved in his great love is the mystery of the unseen perfection and beauty of the human person. The third great mystery underlying Jesus' burning love for us is the mystery of the mystical body.

The beauty of the human body has been hymned in song and legend, and carved into stone and bronze from time immemorial. Yet the body draws all its form and perfection from the human soul and is only a faint image of the soul's purely spiritual beauty.

A three-year-old child can model a horse in clay but he will conceal rather than express the grace and strength of that animal. So, too, even the most perfect human body is as much a mask as a mirror of the beauty of the soul in which it exists. No one on earth can by natural powers see a human soul. We can read a little of the soul's beauty in the body and we can perceive a faint reflection of its more spiritual beauty in the virtues manifested in a person's actions. But Jesus, when he comes in Holy Communion, sees no faint reflections but gazes on the radiant loveliness of the naked soul itself. This is one cause of the love that throbs in his heart when he communicates with us in the Blessed Sacrament.

So far we have spoken of the soul only as it exists in its state of natural virtue and beauty. When Jesus comes he finds it not so. He finds it transformed by baptism into the soul of a divine offspring, a holy and glorious image of God. One of the saints once gazed on such a supernaturally radiant soul and wanted to adore it, thinking it was God. What, then, must be the response of the human heart of Jesus each time he enters through the Eucharist into a human soul?

The third reason why Jesus comes so lovingly in Holy Communion is that he comes not only to a friend, or a beloved; not only to his "brother and sister and mother," but to his very self. He comes to enter into the mystery of his mystical body.

We all love and cherish the members of our own bodies. We treasure the unity we have with each part, we safeguard it, and we seek glowing health for the whole body. Yet, though we love each part of our bodies, the parts do not love us in return. Only where there is knowledge can there be love, and there is no knowledge in our bodily members. It is only the whole person who knows and loves.

With Jesus and his mystical body it is different. He loves and cherishes each member; and each living member loves him in return. Further, when Jesus comes, he knows that the divine life and beauty he beholds in the Christian soul is a communication of his very self: "Just as the living Father sent me, and I live because of the Father, so whoever eats me will live because of me" (John 6:57).

It is to this person with a human nature like his own; to this person made by baptism into an image and likeness of his divinity; to this person living his own life that Jesus comes in Holy Communion. Jesus comes in his exalted divinity; he comes in his pure human soul, and in the radiant body marked with the five wounds, which he has suffered for this very member of himself. Who then can express the love of that eternally wounded heart, beating within that breast, as Jesus comes to claim his own, to unite with his very self? "You have ravished my heart, my sister, my bride" (Song of Solomon 4:9).

The love of the heart of Jesus in Holy Communion is beyond all understanding. Only those with great faith can believe; only those who have received his special favor can begin to know its unplumbed depths.

 Prayer

Let my soul be still, O Jesus, and see that you are God.

Otherwise, I will not know your love, for your love is not only human but divine.

I believe, Jesus, that today in Holy Communion you enter me with that same heart beating in your breast, which was pierced for me on the cross.

I believe you abide in me with that same wounded heart which began to beat anew with love of me on the first Easter morn.

I trust and believe that this reception of your body is a renewed pledge that I shall live forever with your life.

I believe that your heart will beat forever with love of me in heaven, where our communion will continue eternally.

Help me to believe always in your love for me, Jesus, because if I know that you love me so and cherish me as a member of your own body, I will always love you and be faithful to you.

9

---- ✥ ----

EVERLASTING FRUITFULNESS

AS SURELY as the pure mountain spring, sparkling in the sun, draws the thirsty deer from mountain recesses, beauty draws love from the innermost heart of man and woman. Beauty brings forth love; love, union; and union, fruitfulness. At the kiss of the sun, sterile dun fields become nourishing mother earth. The love union of man and wife fructifies in the proliferation of intelligent life. The union of divine and human issues in supernal holiness and the communication of transcendent and eternal life.

These truths in the order of nature and of humanity may help us to see that we can do nothing in the supernatural order unless spiritually united with the divine. "[A]part from me," Jesus asserts with simple directness, "you can do nothing" (John 15:5c). By mind and hand, we children of Adam and Eve can move mountains and empty seas, ascend to the moon and rise to the heavens. But to reach the true heavens, we can't take a step unless the Master of the Heavens first bids us, *Come.* "No one can come to me unless drawn by the Father who sent me," Jesus said (John 6:44). The work of salvation sinks all its roots in the supernatural soil of grace.

By baptism we are planted in the supernatural soil that is Christ. Through union with him we begin living supernaturally, and we receive the vigor to stride swiftly toward a joyous eternity. It is especially in Holy Communion that our life is intensified by direct union with its source, Jesus. Union intensifies love, and this love is charity, the motive power of all holy activity, of all supernatural fruitfulness.

Sometimes gradually, by imperceptible degree, and sometimes with sudden flaming ardor, the one who banquets daily with Jesus is transformed into his strong helper. "Speak, Lord, your servant is listening," is the prayer of the person eagerly poised to set out on the journey into the Lord God's service, whatever the direction and whatever the destination. Once knowing what to do, the lover of Christ says, "Here am I, the servant of the Lord" (Luke 1:38), and rises with haste like Mary to do God's will.

God's will is sweet now, because lover and Beloved have only one will, and it is always pleasant to do one's own will. And ecstatically so, when the loved one is God adored.

"They who have my commandments and keep them," Jesus said "are those who love me" (John 14:21). This is necessarily so, for doing the loved one's will is the irrepressible expression of love. As the sun cannot help but shed its radiance, the will that is one with Jesus' will cannot help but labor with him in everything he says and does that the Father's kingdom may come.

To know exactly what is to be done for Jesus is not always easy. Saint Ignatius Loyola often offered many holy Masses, not to accomplish God's will but just to know it. Knowledge of God's will is a participation in divine wisdom. It is a treasure of great price. The Jews of the Old Testament were immensely proud of the light in which they walked through possession of the Law, while the Gentiles stumbled along in darkness. God will not give this pearl of divine knowledge to those who would only trample it in the mire of their disordered lives. Unless a person is trying sincerely to live according to his lights, it is a mockery of God to ask further directives.

The great directive of the Christian life was given at the Last Supper. "I give you a new commandment, that you love one another. Just as I have loved you, you also should love one another. By this everyone will know that you are my disciples, if you have love for one another" (John 13:34–35).

How this directive is to be expressed today and all the days of our lives is clear from the norms Jesus will follow at the last judgment: "Come, you that are blessed by my Father," our King will say, "inherit the kingdom prepared for you from the foundation of the world; for I was hungry and you gave me food, I was thirsty and you gave me something to drink, I was a stranger and you welcomed me, I was naked and you gave me clothing, I was sick and you took care of me, I was in prison and you visited me" (Matthew 25:34–36). These acts are the supernatural fruitfulness which should issue abundantly from our divine union with Jesus in the love and mystery of Holy Communion. If ever beauty brought forth love; love, union, and union, fruitfulness, what is to be said when the beauty is God's, union is with him, and the fruitfulness flows from his life-giving oneness with us? The world cannot contain the superabundance of this harvest. All eternity will be wealthy with its issue.

Prayer

Divine Jesus, you said that we glorify the Father by bringing forth very much fruit and becoming your disciples in every deed.

I know of your ardent desire to glorify the Father, Jesus, and so I want to bring forth much evidence of my union with you to please you and to glorify God.

Help me, Jesus, to make my every act an act of love for you.

Everything I do, I want to do to you, according to your words, "Truly I tell you, just as you did it to one of the least of these who are members of my family, you did it to me" (Matthew 25:40).

Then, Jesus, I will have the joy of serving you all the day long and of enduring for you the suffering that it will cost to have such a life of faith.

When you see me bring forth such fruit, Jesus, you will know that I am a branch living no life but that which I draw from you, the eternal Vine.

You will know that I am your hands and your Heart, living in the world today.

You will know that everything I do is the fruit of love and union with the divine.

Then, divine Jesus, how greatly you will welcome me in Holy Communion, the fountain of all supernatural fruitfulness!

Divine Jesus, without you I can do nothing.

I long for you.

I hope in you.

Jesus, let me never be confounded.

Little Office of The Holy Name

(from Liber Devotionum Societatis Jesu, 141ff.)

Vespers

Jesus, the very thought of Thee
    With sweetness fills my breast;
But sweeter far Thy face to see,
    And in Thy presence rest.
Nor voice can sing, nor heart can frame,
    Nor can the memory find,
A sweeter sound than Thy blest name,
    O Savior of mankind!
O hope of every contrite heart,
    O joy of all the meek,
To those who fall, how kind Thou art!
    How good to those who seek!
But what to those who find? Ah, this
    Nor tongue nor pen can show:
The love of Jesus, what it is
    None but His loved ones know.
Jesus, our only joy be Thou,
    As Thou our prize wilt be;
Jesus, be Thou our glory now,
    And through eternity.

Matins

O Jesus, king most wonderful,
>   Thou conqueror renowned,
Thou sweetness most ineffable,
>   In whom all joys are found!
When once Thou visitest the heart,
>   Then truth begins to shine;
Then earthly vanities depart;
>   Then kindles love divine.
O Jesus, light of all below,
>   Thou fount of life and fire,
Surpassing all the joys we know,
>   And all we can desire:
May every heart confess Thy name,
>   And ever Thee adore;
And, seeking Thee, itself inflame
>   To seek Thee more and more.
Thee may our tongues forever bless;
>   Thee may we love alone;
And ever in our lives express
>   The image of Thine own.

Lauds

O Jesus, Thou the beauty art
>   Of angel worlds above;
Thy name is music to the heart,
>   Enchanting it with love.
Celestial sweetness unalloyed!
>   Who eat Thee hunger still;

Who drink of Thee still feel a void
    Which naught but Thou can fill.
O my sweet Jesus, hear the sighs
    Which unto Thee I send;
To Thee mine inmost spirit cries
    My being's hope and end!
Stay with us, Lord, and with Thy light
    Illume the soul's abyss;
Scatter the darkness of our night,
    And fill the world with bliss.
O Jesus, spotless virgin flower,
    Our life and joy; to Thee
Be praise, beatitude, and power
    Through all eternity.

PART TWO

Eucharistic Friendship with Jesus Christ

10

IMMENSE JOURNEY

THE COMING TOGETHER of God and man in Holy Communion is the consummation of the most immense journeys ever traveled.

Matching deed to daring concept, Marco Polo trod interminable paths to legendary China. In creaking ships Christopher Columbus ventured into strange new seas and sailed onward in the face of threatened mutiny, starvation, and enmeshment in the chaos of the unknown. At last with unimaginable thrill he set foot on the periphery of a new continent. The legendary Odysseus left the windy plains of Troy to undertake a fabulous journey, that he might at last see again with his eyes and encircle in strong arms his faithfully waiting Penelope. But all these journeys are not in the same league as the wonderful saga of the human journey to God and God's journey to us.

Anthropology, archeology, and revelation, coming to the help of our glimpse of the darkness of prehistory, tell us that only ages of struggle and growth, lent wings at last by the Incarnation, have brought humanity to its current level of consciousness and culture.

And, in a sense and to a degree, each of us repeats the whole human journey. The person who approaches the

Eucharistic Lord is like every other creature who once was not and who one day surged forth from nothingness. The Creator's voice spoke and a new body and soul leaped across the immense void separating nonbeing from being and cried obediently to God, "Here I am, Lord!" On that day a new person crossed the uncrossable abyss which marked the very beginning of an immense journey.

On the day of baptism, Christians traverse the second part of their immense journey. They ascend into the supernatural world, they soar on the wings of grace into a new life unknown until now, a new life and a new nature so much like God's that now they are children of God.

The man, the woman, the child coming forward to receive Holy Communion have come far, but the One meeting them there has come infinitely farther. There is no other journey like the journey from the divine bosom of God, Light of lights, Infinity of infinities, to the tiny human body sleeping in the womb of the Virgin Mary. Infinitely pure Spirit put on flesh and blood like ours. God, whom no one had ever seen, became sensible, visible, tangible. He became small and was a Child held in a Mother's arms. He became a Man and was jostled and pushed; he was kissed and sneered at and struck.

Even then the Son of God had not completed his immense journey. Onward he went, onward and downward through the doors of death to that state of near-nothingness where human soul and body are hewn apart and mortal life is gone.

In the second chapter of his letter to the Philippians, Saint Paul recounts the immense journey of the Son who never left his Father's bosom: "[T]hough he was in the form of God," he "did not regard equality with God as something to be exploited, but emptied himself, taking the form of a slave, being formed in human likeness. And being found in human form, he humbled himself, and became obedient to the point of death—even death on a cross. Therefore God also highly exalted him and gave him the name that is above every name, so that at the name of Jesus every knee should bend, in heaven and on earth and under the earth, and every tongue should confess that Jesus is Lord, to the glory of God the Father" (Philippians 2:6–11).

This immense journey of the loving God, and of the beloved creature, is, all of it, preparation for Holy Communion. Only he whose heart understands such things can possibly know what response to make when, for a moment, the immense journey is ended and the meeting begins.

Prayer

O Eucharistic Journeyer, you are present to me in Holy Communion only because your Father sent you on the immense journey from divine nature into our human nature, and from human life to human death, and upward to the resurrection of your human body. You are the God-Hero Isaiah foretold, the one whom nothing could stop or deter on your determined journey into love and love's victory forever.

And I am present to you in Holy Communion only because of my immense journey to you. Who can tell even that lesser tale! Some of it I don't even know. I was born into this world, not by my own doing, but by yours and my parents. They united in love and you joined your creative act with theirs to give me life and being. For nine months I journeyed into babyhood in my mother's womb, until she gave me birth.

By your loving call and the maternity of Mother Church, I was soon reborn as child of God. One day I had the inexpressible grace of my First Holy Communion. Since, I have traveled the journey of life and fought the battles for goodness and faithfulness, and through the years received you again and again into my heart in loving Communion.

My immense journey is not ended. O, keep me faithful until the Communion with you in heaven that will at last end my journey and assure me that I am home in your Heart forever.

11

TRUST IN JESUS

A TIRED MAN LAY ASLEEP, pillowed against the violent rocking of the boat by the cushions beneath him and by the depths of his human exhaustion. His companions, alarmed by the threatening seas, waked him and cried, "Teacher, do you not care that we are perishing?" (Mark 4:38). The tired man stood, and the breath of his voice quelled the violent winds, and the power of his word made the raging seas become a great calm.

So human is Jesus that sometimes in practice we all but forget that he is divine. Troubles cloud our faith and shake our trust. Though we never wholly lose our faith in Jesus, we, like his disciples, allow both faith and trust to suffer partial eclipse. Lack of trust is a wound to love, and we, like the disciples, must listen to Jesus ask: "Have you still no faith?" (Mark 4:40).

What is the secret of perfect trust in Jesus? Trust stems from a knowledge that another has the power to be able to help us, and the love to extend that help. We will trust perfectly in Jesus when we truly know him in all his divine power and believe in the depths of his divine love for us.

Often, then, when our trust grows dim, it is not precisely that we do not love Jesus; nor is it precisely that we lack belief in his love for us. Our trust grows dim because we do not know Jesus as we ought. If the disciples had known Jesus, need they have feared he was not watching over them simply because he was sleeping? He whose tired body lay asleep in their boat was directing the course of the stars and making the sun send forth its light and creating new life in a million hidden places.

If we fail to search out, by reading and meditation, the mystery of the person of Jesus, our trust in him will certainly suffer. It is not enough simply to believe that Jesus is divine as well as human. By reading and by meditation we must look and see that he is God. In our mind's eye, we must see the Son of God with the Father and Holy Spirit working the work of creation by which they made time begin and caused the stars to flare into being all across the universe. We must see them creating the beloved angels, and forming the body of the first man, and breathing into it a life they intended to keep burning forever—if only man would not sin. We must see the Son of God, together with his Father and Holy Spirit, guiding the destiny of the earth, calling Abraham, giving him Isaac; leading Isaac to the well to meet beautiful Rebecca, all in preparation for the day the Virgin Mary would say "Yes!" to her vocation, and the Son would be clothed in his garment of flesh and dwell among us.

Even the knowledge that Jesus is really God, with all the power of God, is not enough. Nor is it enough to know that he is also man. We can know these things, and still not trust him enough. We must know his ways. We must understand his absolute hatred of sin and his inexhaustible compassion for sinners. We must know that he has come and placed peace in our hearts but a sword in our hands. When trials, shattering temptations, sickness and disappointment strike, we will find our trust badly shaken unless we have come to understand Jesus and have learned the ways of our God. To those whom he loves most he frequently gives a double share in his own sufferings, just as he will give them a double portion of his victory. In Adam, man was struck to the earth by Satan. In Christ man has stood again, and renewed the combat, and in Christ all who want to share the victory must carry on the fight. Until we know this, we will not understand Christ and his ways.

This is a terrible lesson and terribly hard to learn. Even the Saints mastered the lesson only with great difficulty. Even such a Saint as Catherine of Siena found it hard. Burning with love for Jesus, she was not only ready but eager to suffer and wear herself out and die for love of him. But the suffering of temptation was a different matter. One day, when the devil came and tempted her with unclean thoughts which she abhorred, she was deeply hurt that Christ should permit such a thing. Afterward, she complained to Jesus and asked why he had abandoned her. Jesus assured her he had not abandoned her. He explained that his presence during the temptation was the only reason she could resist it.

When temptations are endured in Jesus, they are only preludes to victory. Only as such does his love permit them.

Knowledge of Jesus spreads peace in the midst of spiritual war, sustains confidence in the midst of disaster and is a fountain of hope that will spring up to perfect fulfillment. The war will be no less real and the blood that is shed will still be true blood. The disaster will be real and the suffering will darken the mind and stagger the will; but knowledge and love of Jesus are rooted deep in the soul and, if they are healthy, their flower of trust will survive every ordeal.

Prayer

Divine Jesus, let me never look on you with that distrustful eye that rends your heart like the soldier's lance on Calvary. Give me that bottomless trust in you that was such a joy to your Heart while you lived on earth.

Give me, my Lord and Savior, the determination to take the means to grow in trust of you. Help me resolve to do what is necessary to gain the knowledge and understanding of you that are the necessary foundations of an unshakable trust. One of your own commands, Jesus, is "Learn of Me." And the one who keeps your commands, Jesus, is the one who loves you. I want to be one who keeps your commands, learns of you and comes to trust you completely.

My only Lord and Savior Jesus Christ, make my soul such a deep ocean of trust in you that no trial and no storm of temptation can ever disturb its placid depths. Give me, O Jesus, the trust in you which I long for, and trust that you will give me.

Mary, Mother of fair love, you trusted your Son in everything and through everything, even the disgrace and disaster of Calvary. How your Son must have admired and appreciated your trust! Look on me and see how earnestly I ask for, and count on, you to inspire me by your example, and help me by your prayers, so that I too will maintain a noble trust in him. Win for me the grace that whenever he comes to me in Holy Communion, he will be consoled by the trust in him that I never abandon.

12

———— 〜 ————

FAITH IN JESUS

FAITH IS A SUBSTITUTE for vision. The very ring of the word "substitute" leaves us with an empty feeling. We want the genuine article. We take on faith what scientists tell us about the atom and what doctors tell us of our bodies, but we remain unsatisfied. We want to see for ourselves. Even faith in Jesus labors under this disadvantage. Only here there is a wonderful compensation. To believe in Jesus is to accept not a man's knowledge but God's knowledge in place of our own. In other words, belief in Jesus is in itself part of our supernatural union with Jesus. Belief in Jesus is, in fact, the foundation of that union. "The one who believes and is baptized will be saved; but the one who does not believe will be condemned" (Mark 16:16).

Faith, even in Jesus, is not easy. Not even the blind like to be led. The spirit of independence rebels against it. The spirit of fear distrusts it.

Once a little boy stood on a wharf in pitch blackness. In the overcast night, the eerie splashing of the waves against the boat below was a disembodied sound. From out of the darkness beneath came the strong sound of his father's voice: "You can't see me, son, but I can see you. Jump and I'll catch you." Fear clutched at the child's heart, all but routing the untroubled confidence of filial love. He hesitated—he leaped—and the strong arms of his father gathered the boy to his bosom.

Similarly, faith, even in Jesus, demands heroic trust. Yet love casts out fear, and the belief that cuts us loose from dependence on the sounds and sights of earth puts us in the waiting arms of God.

The simplest way to grow in the faith Jesus demands is to grow in the love of Jesus. Love casts out fear. Love seeks union, not independence. Love thrills to the true meaning of faith. Faith in Jesus is nothing but the surrender to him by which we begin to see with the eyes of Jesus.

 ## Prayer

O Jesus, what a privilege faith is! By faith I share your divine and human vision. I share the very light of your eyes. Even now you look on God, and are God. By faith I share in the knowledge of what you see, and I say, "There are three Persons in one God." By faith in you I share in the secrets of God's heart and I say, "You have loved me and delivered yourself up for me!" By faith I accept the authority of your word, and in reward God the Father accepts me as his child and you accept me as part of your very self, a member of your body. Faith joins me to you in loving surrender.

Increase my faith in your Real Presence in Holy Communion, Jesus, so that through your eyes I see you present to me even as you promised to be in the sacrament of the Eucharist. Make my faith so living that when I receive you today I may love you with all my heart.

Deepen my faith, my Lord, that I may see clearly with your eyes and hear clearly with your ears. Deepen my faith and my union with you hour by hour until that day of days when, through my perfect oneness with you, all darkness is dispersed and in the eternal noon I see my God face to face.

13

———— ❧ ————

LOVING JESUS BY FAITH

WE DO NOT KNOW how to love Jesus as we ought with all-embracing supernatural love; Yet Jesus knows the love we owe him and he desires to receive our love. There is a way we can love Jesus as we ought, without knowing how. We must go by the dark road of faith. "The one who is righteous will live by faith," as the scriptures teach (Romans 1:17). Our love for Jesus must be offered to him in the wrappings of faith.

Like a bold explorer launching off into trackless wastes in search of new lands and new treasures, we must launch ourselves blindly into the works of love which faith requires. Only in the making of the journey does the explorer learn where the journey leads. Only in doing the works of faith which love of Jesus requires do we come by imperceptible degrees to solving the mystery of how we should love Jesus. In the supernatural order as well as in the natural order, we must often learn by doing.

We can find our way along the dark road of faith by following in the tracks of Jesus and by obeying his teaching. In particular, he gave us his new commandment. We must love one another as he has loved us. He gave us both the reason and the effect of such love when he illumined us with the blinding light of a new revelation: "What you do unto others, you do unto Me."

All our loves must be charged with a new tenderness in the light of this new truth. The Christian father and mother must embrace their little sons and daughters with a love like God's own, for they are members of the body of Jesus. In loving their children, parents are loving God's and Mary's Son. Husband and wife find in one another the image of God; in their family they see the image of the Trinity and in their union an expression of the mystical union of Christ with his members.

We must learn to love our parents as images of God, who is the true source of our being, and as images of Jesus, who gave us new supernatural being by giving us rebirth in his mystical body.

We learn to love Jesus not only in our family relationships but in our friendships and our meetings with strangers. What we do unto all others, we do unto Christ. When we show compassion by visiting a sick friend or when we are generous to a needy family, it is Jesus who is consoled by our visit and whose needs are assuaged by our gifts. "Truly I tell you, just as you did it to one of the least of these who are members of my family, you did it to me" (Matthew 25:40).

Not only human beings but all other things must be treasured for the sake of Jesus. The food we eat must remind us of the only true Bread, Jesus himself. It should not be so difficult to realize Jesus is the only true Bread, since nothing exists or has goodness except through him, and anything one of his creatures does for us he can do more personally, and with infinitely greater sweetness and power. Does the ground beneath our feet support us and the air sustain our life and the sun warm us and our food nourish us? The day is coming when he will be our Earth and our Air, our Sun and our Food. Of food Jesus has already said: "Very truly, I tell you, unless you eat the flesh of the Son of Man and drink his blood, you have no life in you. Those who eat my flesh and drink my blood have eternal life, and I will raise them up on the last day" (John 6:53–54).

Is it so difficult to realize what Jesus, Emmanuel, God with us, should mean to us? Is it so difficult to understand the love we owe him and to offer that love? He who gave us all things must be more to us than all he gave us. He who gave us mother and sister and brother must be more to us than mother and sister and brother. He must not only be more to us than all else; he must be all to us, and all else must be loved because in some way it is Jesus to us.

Yet clear as all this is, we shall never really understand it unless we live it. It is only by doing the truth that we can know the truth. Only those who live the truth can understand Jesus, the Living Truth.

 ## Prayer

When shall I see the face of my God? Jesus, how long must I find you in many faces and many voices, before I can look into your face and hear your voice? Jesus, I love you enough to continue to give you my love by giving it to others. I love you enough to work for you by working for the members of your body. I long for your love enough to penetrate the impersonal face of nature, and so find your veiled presence and your love for me in the food that nourishes me, the clothing that covers me, the sun that warms me. I find your love for me in the friend who brings hours of joy into my life.

Above all, I find you in Holy Communion by faith in your word that you yourself come to me in your flesh and blood. When the Holy Spirit moves me, I commune with you ardently, and am at times full of consolation and joy and deep happiness in the sense of your Real Presence and the pleasure of your companionship, in the banquet of love.

Yet in all these ways I find you obscured by shadows. I will seek you amid shadows as long as you want me to, my Jesus, but I long to see your face, O my God.

14

RELATIONSHIP WITH JESUS

Our relationship to Jesus is a profound mystery that has not yet fully appeared except in signs and mysterious symbols. The reason for this is not solely that Jesus himself is a deep mystery to us: he who is Man, yet not a human but a divine Person; he who is Man, Son of Mary, yet no longer mortal like us, but the risen, transformed, eternally life-filled Son of Man. The reason why our relation to Jesus is such a profound mystery extends to ourselves. We no longer know what we are.

Baptism has transported us into another world, the world of the invisible divine Trinity, the angels and the saints. Baptism gave us birth not of man and woman "but of God." We are now *tekna Theou,* children of God. What does this mean? We can't yet know fully what it means to be children of God. Saint John speaks of the day when "we will be like him, for we will see him as he is" (1 John 3:2). On that day when we see God, we shall for the first time come to see and fully know ourselves, *tekna Theou.*

But this much we do know even now, that there is only one way to become children of God, and that is to be "plunged into Christ," the only Son of God. So Saint Paul teaches (see Galatians 3:27), and in like manner Jesus himself speaks. "I am the vine, you the branches" (John 15:5a). The one broken off this vine is dead, useless for anything but the fire. Saint John even gives us a measure to show we have been begotten of God, and are not broken off the vine: "If you know that he is righteous, you may be sure that everyone who does right has been born of him" (1 John 2:29).

Not only do we begin our true life by this mysterious union with Jesus but we live on in holiness only by continued communion with him. He is the true bread. We cannot live on eternally except by the bread of his flesh, as we know he taught. He is also the true light of our minds and hearts. These are only some of the signs and symbols which have begun the revelation of our mysterious relationship to Jesus.

The reason our relationship to Jesus is so cloaked in mystery is that it is altogether supernatural. The supernatural is the realm of faith, not of clear knowledge. Yet we are given hints of the nature of our relationship with Jesus through the signs and symbols already mentioned. Like Mary, we must ponder these things in our hearts. We are the branches, Jesus the Vine. He is our life. We are the body of Jesus. What do these things mean? The Holy Spirit is eager to give us deeper insights, if only we will pray over these holy truths.

Jesus has made it plain to us that we can't yet fully understand what he is to us or what we are to him: "Whoever does the will of God, he is my brother and sister and mother." These are not mere words for the sake of words. They are flashes of fire from the lips of Jesus that illumine for a moment the mysterious realities of another world, the world of the simplicity of the one God, who is all in all. Of that world, by the love of Jesus, we now have a share.

Prayer

Divine Savior, Jesus, my Lord and my Life, it is when you speak in the Gospels and I listen that I hear distant echoes of the divine answer to my deepest longings. I long and long to be carried by the embrace of my God beyond the slightest danger and shadow of sin to a land of eternal union with him. Sin separates me from you, my God, sin wounds our mutual love, and you know the suffering it causes me when I fail in my love for you, and feel your love for me distanced by barriers of my own making. I long to be so united with my God that sin is immeasurably far below us, in a world that is separated from us by a great chasm, so it can never interfere with our union again.

When I listen to you, Jesus, I hear from your own Heart that my longings are only the echoes of your own great longings. You have prepared for us a marvelous world where these longings will be forever satisfied because perfect union with our God will be found. You have prepared a world without Satan and without sin. You have prepared heaven for us.

In Holy Communion, the promise and foretaste of heaven begin to reveal to my soul the joys that await us, O Jesus, that your joy may be in me and my joy may be made full in you.

15

THE VISION OF GOD

NO ONE HAD ever seen God. Until Jesus opened the gates of heaven, no one had ever seen God, except the Son who from all eternity rested on the breast of the Father.

Even during his earthly life, the human soul of Jesus was in direct communion with God. Even then, while his body and his Heart shared our sorrows, his human soul saw always his own divinity and the divinity of his Father and their Holy Spirit.

Jesus came to earth to share with us his knowledge of God.

The human nature of Jesus is a translucent veil transmitting the glory of God, softening God's glory to fit our gaze. Jesus was hurt when Philip failed to realize this, failed to find the Father in him. "Have I been with you all this time, Philip, and you still do not know me? Whoever has seen me has seen the Father" (John 14:9). Jesus is the visible image of the invisible God. People could look on him as they can gaze on the crimson glory in the East, early, before the flaming sun rises up and compels all eyes to turn away.

In Holy Communion Jesus can share with us another, deeper knowledge of God than that which people gained by gazing on his human form. True, only in heaven will we be given the power to see God face to face. But when Jesus comes to us in Holy Communion, he is like an explorer returned from unknown lands, able to share with others all that he has seen. Jesus' human soul sees God, and can communicate to our souls, in human terms, something of the knowledge and the torrent of delight that the vision of God brings. Without words or images or visions Jesus can communicate to our minds a deeper knowledge of God and to our hearts a love beyond all measure.

There are no secrets between friends. While our souls are immersed in the Soul of Jesus during Holy Communion, he is more than willing to whisper with unheard words these secrets to those who have made their hearts pure enough to see God. "So I tell you, whatever you ask for in prayer, believe that you have received it, and it will be yours" (Mark 11:24).

There is no more favorable time to gain this deeper knowledge of Jesus than during our communing with his Real Presence. The mystic and doctor of the Church, Saint Teresa of Avila, reports in her *Spiritual Testimonies of Jesus* that "From certain things he told me, I understood that after he ascended into heaven he never came down to earth to commune with anyone except in the most Blessed Sacrament" (12).

Pope Pius XII, who knew so well the tender Heart of Jesus, assured us in his encyclical on the Mystical Body that the Savior longs to speak with each single member of his Body, "heart to heart, especially after Holy Communion." It is not hard to know what he wants to speak of. We cannot tell him anything of ourselves that he doesn't already know, but like all lovers he rejoices when we tell him of our love and hopes and prayers. Surely it is clear that if we so long to be known by him that we repeat to him what he already knows of us, he too must long to reveal himself to us. He must long to be unknown to us no longer. "Listen! I am standing at the door, knocking; if you hear my voice and open the door, I will come in to you and eat with you, and you with me" (Revelation 3:20).

In Holy Communion Jesus does long to share with us, in the deepest possible measure, his vision of God. It is his very Heart's desire, for he longs to have us know him, and he is God.

Prayer

Jesus, I long to know you even as I long to be known by you. Jesus, I lay my soul bare to you, with all its sins and wounds of sin. I desire to hide none of them from you, Jesus, for I know your love is great enough to forgive them all. Your love is so great, Jesus, that you come, not to blame me, but to console me.

But I desire too to know you, whom I have never seen. Have pity on my ignorance of you after having been with you so long a time, Jesus. How long shall I walk in blindness at your side, O Light of the World? Take away the shame of my blindness even as you cleanse me from the shame of my sins. "Lord, that I may see!" In Holy Communion, my beloved Savior, communicate to my quiet soul a knowledge of you, whom I have longed and longed to see. Amen.

16

—— ≋ ——

JESUS, OUR SACRIFICE

OFFERING JESUS to God in the Eucharistic Sacrifice is the central act of our worship, to which we were consecrated by Jesus himself. It is the most significant work of a lifetime. Only here and on the hill of Calvary is our eternal salvation brought to pass. Offering the Lamb of God to God should bring our greatest peace and our greatest joy. If it brings neither it may be because we have not penetrated the mystery of the Mass and learned to offer Jesus as we ought.

How can anyone join the priest in offering the sacrifice of the Mass well until he really understands what he is offering, until he really knows Jesus for what he is and what he has done, and loves him beyond all measure? A little child may unwittingly exchange an old dollar bill for a shiny penny; a man unaware of the gold mine hidden in his field may sell the land for a pittance. We may similarly lack wisdom in the way we offer Jesus to the Father. If we knew the gift we offered, and offered it with love, we would no longer hesitate to ask all things in return. In fact, we would be ashamed of asking too little of the Father in return for the Sacrifice of Jesus. To offer the Son of God in sacrifice and ask a trifle in return is foolish, if not insulting to Jesus.

We cannot gain this knowledge of Jesus overnight. Even human friendship cannot develop in a moment. How much less can any brief period bring to maturity a friendship which is spiritual and supernatural, one in which the Friend offers his life for our redemption, and plunges us into the divine abyss of God's own beauty and love?

Yet in some Christians, even frequent communicants, this friendship seems to mature hardly at all. Far from being charged with the thunder of the seas, far from unfolding with the vitality of a bursting bud, their relationship with Jesus seems a static thing. In such a case, one should question the sincerity of one's efforts to grow in the knowledge and love and service of Jesus. For God has so made us that our love goes out to whatever we know that is good, and deepening knowledge of Jesus will mean deepening love, unless we are hardening our hearts to the demands of Jesus.

Christians who make a realistic effort to know better the Light of the World will surely be given what they seek. And as they penetrate the boundless depths of the glorious Person of Jesus, their love will burst into flame like straw cast on the furnace of the sun.

Since in offering the Holy Sacrifice, we offer the whole life and person of Jesus, we ought to familiarize ourselves with that life. This will take us to the four Gospels. By meditating over the truths found there, and by conversing with Jesus personally in prayer, we will gain the knowledge and love we need to offer Mass well.

At Bethlehem we will learn the meaning of the words of Isaiah: "A child is born to us, and a Son is given to us." We will grow in the realization that Jesus really is ours to offer to God. He has come to earth in order to be ours.

When we meditate on Jesus calming the skies and the seas with a gesture; when in his prayer we behold Jesus standing alive and well before Thomas with a wound that cleaved open his beating heart, we will learn to cry in a new way, with Thomas, "My Lord and my God!" (John 20:28).

When we gaze at the bloody sweat of Jesus that tells how hard Jesus found it to sacrifice himself, we will find new meaning in the Mass. When in repeated meditations we stand with the grief-stricken Virgin Mother on Calvary and learn what the Holy Sacrifice really is, we will be ready to offer the Sacrifice worthily. To watch Jesus suffering torture, to watch the lifeblood drain from his body, makes it impossible ever again to offer the Sacrifice of Calvary in the same old uninvolved way.

After we live through Jesus' suffering with him by many days of meditation, we may find that the Holy Sacrifice seems far too great a price to pay for the salvation of lowly creatures like us. The words of Peter come to mind: "Go away from me, Lord, for I am a sinful man!" (Luke 5:8). How can the Christian callously offer so divine a Gift to buy back his worthless self? Now he begins to understand the love of God his Father for him, a love that offered up the only-begotten Son to such redemptive sufferings on his behalf. Before such a flood of the Creator's love he is compelled to exclaim: "Father, if I must offer Jesus up to such torture, at least take me with him on the way of suffering!" And to the crucified Jesus he speaks tenderly:

These wounds, my Lord, Thou makest Thine.
Share them with me, for they are mine.

Then comes to pass what God has willed all along. God wants not only the Gift but the giver. And now both are offered to him as one, in the unity of love, in the unity of the Mystical Body of Christ. This unity of suffering with Jesus is completed and transcended by unity with him in joy and life. This too comes about through the mystery of the Eucharist. For when we offer the Sacrificial Lamb to the Father, the Father does not take him from us forever, but shares him with us at once in the banquet of Holy Communion. We offer Jesus in his dying and his coming to life and his eternal glory, and we receive him glorious and immortal in the food that brings eternal life and fellowship with him.

Offering the Holy Sacrifice does not take Jesus from us but takes us to Jesus, and with him to God the Father, and there unites us with Jesus forever. When we understand these things, the Sacrifice of Jesus becomes the central action of our lives. The Mass becomes filled with the long sorrow of the crucifixion of Jesus and the eternal joy of the resurrection of Jesus. It becomes the moment of eternal gift-giving, we continually offering Jesus to God the Father and he forever sharing Jesus with us. In this immaculate Sacrifice and sacred Banquet we find our fusion with God in Christ Jesus.

Prayer

Divine Jesus, what if I were to offer you to the Father and he were to accept my gift, and take you from me forever? Let this terrible thought, Jesus, bring home to me the emptiness of a redemption that would not include fellowship with you. Let it impress on me the goodness of God our Father in making Holy Communion our privilege at every Holy Sacrifice. The Father does not want to separate you from us. He accepts you from our hands to join us to you always.

My Savior, help me to realize what I am really doing when I join the priest in offering you to the Father in the Holy Sacrifice of the Mass. The *Catechism of the Catholic Church* tries to bring it home to me in telling me that "When the Church celebrates the Eucharist, she commemorates Christ's Passover, and it is made present: the sacrifice Christ offered once for all on the cross remains ever present" (1364). We know you don't suffer anew, Lord, but you continue to offer everything you offered on the Cross for us: "In the Eucharist Christ gives us the very body which he gave up for us on the cross, the very blood which he 'poured out for many for the forgiveness of sins'" (1365). Many Saints have learned to think of you on the Cross whenever they offer Mass, to appreciate how much you loved us, and to be moved to love you in return.

For my part, at every Eucharist I want to be aware that I am accepting from you all that you suffered on the Cross to redeem me. I want that realization to make me ready and even eager to undergo my share of your redemptive sufferings in my life, Jesus. Make me ashamed of anything less. Can I say yes to your death for me on Calvary while I continue to concentrate on the pleasures of this mortal life?

May the longing to be with you always and never to be parted from you make me ready and even eager to suffer whatever unites me more closely to You, Jesus my Savior. I want always to be on the paten with you, offered with you to the Father for my sins and the sins of all. Amen.

17

THE PRESENCE OF JESUS

THE FIRST LONGING OF LOVE is for the presence of the beloved. Lovers proverbially manifest undreamed of wisdom and the endurance of saints to gain the presence of the loved one. But when the one who loves is Jesus, the wisdom ascends to the realms of the ineffable and the longing is an everlasting song of love.

If we wish to contemplate and cherish the first moment when Jesus sought us out in love, we must travel in spirit back to a day when we were not yet conceived in our mother's womb and back to a time before the Word became flesh of the Virgin Mary. Before the world sprouted up like a seed from the hand of its Creator, and before the first cherubim and seraphim hid their eyes from the splendor of God, he who would one day deliver himself up for us had already sought us out and planned to create us, taking pity on us in his love. "Therefore I have drawn thee, taking pity on thee" (Jeremiah 31:3, Douai–Rheims).

As a sculptor loves the vision within him even before he immortalizes it in stone, the Holy Trinity have eternally cherished the divine idea of us which existed in them before the world was. From all eternity the Son has known us and loved us, though we had not even come to be. And as knowledge is part of the knower, this image of us was part of God. He knew us in knowing himself.

Together with his eternal knowledge of us, the divine Son had eternal knowledge of countless other creatures he could have made, could have given a created share of his own divine perfection. Many of these other possible creatures were incomparably more perfect and lovable than we, yet in the mystery of his predilection he chose to love us and to decree from all eternity that he would one day make us to be and to forever share his love. The haunting beauty of the creatures, which could have been but never will be, tells us the more of the greatness of his love for us whom he has loved with his everlasting love.

This knowledge and love of us which God has always had for us compelled him to come to us in his great compassion. He who made us made himself a man for us. "[T]he Word became flesh and lived among us" (John 1:14). He who had put us outside of himself, as it were, by creating us, rejoined us and gathered us to his bosom by coming to be one of us and dwelling among us, for as the Scriptures tell us, he delights to be with us. He came, not to bring sorrow but to be the Man of Sorrows, and thus bring joy; he came, not to exact justice, but by fulfilling justice in his own body, to bring love.

All the days of his life the Son of Mary carried us about in his human heart because we were ever present to his mind's eye. "Can a woman forget her nursing child, or show no compassion for the child of her womb? Even these may forget, yet I will not forget you" (Isaiah 49:15). He could never forget us, this Jesus who has known us from all eternity and who in the fullness of time emptied himself and took the form of a slave to be with us and to take us to himself. Even the thousand needles of agony which pierced his body on Calvary could not change his love for us. Even the cold black waves of death which mounted up against him and robbed the warmth of life from his wounded heart could not extinguish his love for us. It is true that for three days his human heart ceased to beat with love for us, but even during those days in which his body lay cold in the earth, we lived on in his human soul as we have forever been present to his divinity. Because his love was stronger than death, he rose again, and ascended to his Father. And now in heaven the divine love of us finds unflagging new expression in the breast of Jesus. His thought is ever of us as he makes intercession before the Father.

One day away from the beloved is as a thousand years. Is thought of the beloved sufficient or does it not rather make pain of separation even more unendurable? Jesus the divine lover is not satisfied with the remembrance of us in his heart. Like the lover of the Canticle, he leaps the mountains of space and skips over the hills of time to be with us, wherever we may be. "Those who love me will keep my word, and my Father will love them, and we will come to them and make our dwelling with them" (John 14:23). Though a man should travel to the farthermost rim of the sea, though he ascend to the planets of the heavens, Jesus would be there to greet him as "brother" and "friend." The three divine Persons who have loved us with an everlasting love could not leave us alone for the greatness of their love. The Son of God has already begun his eternal communion with us and nothing but the gross unfaithfulness of mortal sin will drive him from our souls.

The atmosphere in which we live is a shoreless sea that bathes us within and without. It surrounds us on all sides, it even rushes into the depths of our breast. The air is a symbol of Jesus, whose love urges him to be present to us in every conceivable way.

One of the triumphs of the wisdom of his compelling love is his Mystical Body. In the mystery of baptism, Jesus has created a supernatural unity of Christians with himself that exceeds human understanding. "I am the vine, you are the branches" (John 15:5a). It is a union as real as that which binds together the members of the human body, yet as hidden as the sun in the black of night. In each of these members of his body, Jesus lives and breathes among us. Through them he is present to us in love but through them he is also present to us as a trial. Not as the adorable Son of God who must win our heart without a struggle does he appear to us then, but "as the most despised and abject of men." Only the fire of burning love can dispel this darkness and find Jesus.

Above all ways in this life, Jesus comes to us in his real presence, in his human nature, as truly as he was with Mary. That heart, which beats with love for us in heaven even now, must come and beat within our hearts. That human soul, so overcome with love for the divine image which his own mercy has created in our souls, cannot rest until it rests in us. Jesus has longed and longed for the eucharistic banquet with us. Even this, his human presence, is Jesus compelled by his love to grant us here on earth. He must be totally ours and we totally his. The feel and taste of the bread and wine must say to our faith the words Jesus spoke after his resurrection to followers who thought him a ghost: "[S]ee that it is I myself" (Luke 24:39). Now he is present body and blood, soul and divinity. "I have found him whom my soul loves. I will hold him and will not let him go." This is the fullness of his earthly presence. For more we must wait for that eternal morning rising when "we will be like him, for we will see him as he is" (1 John 3:2). Then at last will we understand and adore the presence by which we are one with Jesus in the bosom of the Holy Trinity.

 ## Prayer

O Jesus, by this do I know that you are God. None but God could have such love and no other could find so many ways of encompassing us about and filling us with his presence. Divine Lord, my soul's bridegroom, let me not be so ungracious and ungrateful as to frequently and coldly refuse to engage in the prayerful communion with you to which your presence within me through the day is always inviting me. In prayer I need not cry out to you in the far-off heavens, for I have learned from you that the kingdom of heaven is within me. Like Mary's prayer, my prayer will not be a loud cry but an unspoken communing with you in my heart.

Above all, Jesus, give me the opportunity and the grace of being united with you daily in Holy Communion. You have crossed eternity to come to me. Call me by your grace and your love and I will cross every barrier that separates me from daily Communion with you. My divine Savior and eternal Lord, call me and I will come to you and learn the secrets of your Sacred Heart. Like the thief on the cross who stole your love, I ask not what I deserve but what I hope in your name, O Jesus.

PART THREE

The King's Sacrament

INTRODUCTION

JESUS CHRIST CREATED FOR US the seven mysteries we know as the seven sacraments. We call them mysteries because what happens when a sacrament is received transcends not only the eye's vision but also the mind's. They are mysteries of faith that transport us into another world.

The theologian says that the sacraments effect what they signify. What is outwardly done by the one administering the sacrament is inwardly done by God in a more spiritual and mysterious manner.

Consider baptism and the meaning of the water used. In the natural order, we come to birth out of water, are washed in water, and can even lose our lives by an inundation of water. The water of baptism is a symbol of all these events in the spiritual order. The one baptizing pours water on the person, or even immerses the person in water, while saying the words that Christ requires. In consequence, the baptized person dies with Christ to the sinful way of life begun by Adam, is washed and cleansed of all sin, and comes forth from the water to a new birth and new life with and in Christ.

In like manner each of the other sacraments involves an action which is a symbol and a cause of some supernatural effect neither seen nor fully understood.

All the sacraments bring us grace; in doing so they bring us closer to God, the source of all grace. The sacraments are seven doors to God. If this be true of all seven sacraments, how much more is it true of the Holy Eucharist! It contains not only the door to God but God himself! Under the fragile appearances of bread and wine the risen Jesus is present body and blood, soul and divinity. All the sacraments belong to Christ the King, but this sacrament which contains him is in a special way The King's Sacrament.

The King present is King by right of birth, though he said to Pilate, "My kingdom is not from this world" (John 18:36). In the King's sacrament, Jesus exercises his power as King of kings by bestowing to the communicant the gift of life, eternal life. "Those who eat my flesh and drink my blood have eternal life, and I will raise them up on the last day" (John 6:54). Jesus transmits life to us by a mystic union with his own person that gives a created participation in the joy of God himself.

Jesus won a second title. He is King by right of conquest. His is a conquest of goodness over sin, of love over hatred. Jesus is King by title of conquering love, and the Eucharist is the enduring perpetuation of both his conquest and his love.

The Eucharist is the perpetuation of Jesus' conquest, for it is the heart of the sacramental sacrifice, the Mass. Christ becomes Eucharistically present in the Mass when the priest pronounces the words that offer Jesus to God according to the sacrificial sacrament that Jesus instituted. We can have

Jesus with us Eucharistically only by renewing, in the mystery of the Mass, the sacrifice in which he overcame the world.

The Eucharist perpetuates Jesus' love for the human race by renewing his self-giving for us and extending his self-giving to us. The love of Christ conquers our love not only because he died for us, but because he died to be ours. The Eucharistic sacrifice of the Last Supper was completed by the bloody sacrifice of the next day; but the bloody sacrifice in turn finds in the Eucharistic sacrifice of the night before the means of distributing the graces won. The life which Jesus' death would bring was already promised there; and the union with God which the separation of Jesus' body and blood was destined to bring us was already begun there in that banquet. And it was a banquet. From the moment of that sacrificial banquet the wedding feast of the Lamb has begun.

The love of Jesus at the Last Supper is the love of the Man of Sorrows, but it is also the love that is greater than man's. It is the love of the Author of Life. It is the love of our Lord and King reaching us today in all its vital power, unchecked by the centuries, in the King's Sacrament.

18

---- ❧ ----

THE TENDERNESS OF GOD

GOD IS A RADIANT GLORY. So easily are we over-whelmed by God's power and majesty that we forget the tenderness of God. Yet all human tenderness was created by God, and is less than one drop of the ocean of his tenderness.

How was God to obscure the blinding glory of his majesty so that we might see his tenderness unveiled? God knew the way. He sent his Son clothed in our nature. In Gerard Manley Hopkins' memorable phrase, the humanity of Jesus "sifts God's light to suit our sight." Jesus, "the weakness of God," purposely conceals the divine glory to place more clearly before our eyes the tenderness of God. The Incarnation of his beloved Son put God's exquisite tender-ness within our grasp to be loved, even though it would be wounded by our malice.

At the opening of the human race's long history of sin God cursed the snake which tempted Eve and the ground from which the tree of the forbidden fruit grew, but the man and woman who committed the sin he did not curse. Yet more, in the very hour of their sin he promised them a Savior and clothed their naked bodies with clothing he himself prepared as though to symbolize the future clothing of their souls with the grace of Jesus.

Human arrogance stands in grotesque contrast to the tenderness of God. For men and women, on accession to power, often force their will on others, while the God of all power chooses to win us by his unguarded tenderness. When the devil tempted Jesus to employ the seductive way of power he heard the words: "[I]t is written, 'Do not put the Lord your God to the test'" (Matthew 4:7). No one is capable of tempting God to abandon the ways of his tenderness.

The Pharisees registered shock at Jesus' habit of associating with sinners, only to be told: "Those who are well have no need of a physician, but those who are sick; I have come to call not the righteous but sinners" (Mark 2:17).

To Jesus the sinner is frail as a bruised reed which harsh treatment might break for good. The sinner's ability to love may be as near to extinction as fire in flax that gives off only a wisp of smoke. Can the icy gale of threats help such a one? Our good Shepherd restores love by his tender care: "Come to me, all you that are weary and are carrying heavy burdens, and I will give you rest. Take my yoke upon you, and learn from me; for I am gentle and humble in heart, and you will find rest for your souls. For my yoke is easy, and my burden is light" (Matthew 11:28–30).

The tenderness of God is manifest not only in Jesus' human acts, but in the human violence to which Jesus submitted. Because he did not enforce his rights his body finally lay upon the rock of Calvary lacerated and dead. "From the sole of the foot even to the head there is no soundness in it, but bruises and sores and bleeding wounds" (Isaiah 1:6). The cruelness of men had wounded and slain the tenderness of God.

The tenderness of God is manifest in Jesus, and manifest forever. No one is capable of tempting God to abandon his ways of tenderness. In Holy Communion Jesus the victim comes with a tenderness which, if possible, is greater than ever.

 ## Prayer

O Jesus my Lord let nothing tempt you from your way of tenderness. See the wounds and scars of my sins and heal all with your tender care. Make your yoke sweet to me and your burden light.

I promise in turn, my beloved Lord, to remember your tenderness and to try to be most loving and sinless. It was foreknowledge of my sins that grieved you so heavily in your agony, and it was to wash my sins away that your body was wounded and your blood shed. Now, Divine Love, I want to put into the hand of the strengthening angel of your agony the cup of the wine of my love. I will act toward others as toward you for they are your Body and their frailty is yours. And I will wait to hear with joy from your lips that I have guarded your tenderness. My Lord and King, I want to hear with my own ears from your own lips the words: "[J]ust as you did it to one of the least of these who are members of my family, you did it to me" (Matthew 25:40). Until then, my dear Redeemer, I will try to receive you in Holy Communion with that tenderness with which Mary took your slain body into her arms on Calvary.

19

INDICTMENT OF WICKEDNESS

WRITTEN ON A SIGN hanging above the crucified Son of God was the indictment of his "wickedness": He had claimed to be King. But by crucifying Jesus, we, the human race, wrote in cruel wounds inflicted upon the body of Jesus the indictment of our own human wickedness: by our sins we killed the "Author of life" (Acts 3:15).

In the Garden of Eden the first couple had attempted to displace God by destroying his transcendent authority. On Calvary people tried to forget God by raging against his tenderness, which was an Incarnation of his love.

When, after destroying the innocent, wickedness is compelled to gaze on what it has done it at last comes face to face with its own horror. Jesus is the Innocent One in whom the truth about my sinfulness hangs before my eyes. What I have done or am capable of doing through mortal sin, Jesus crucified reveals to me. Mortal sin attempts to destroy God's sovereignty. But since without sovereignty he is not God, my sin is an attempt to destroy God in my life. The state of the lost is everlasting success.

Until I see in the cruelness destroying Jesus on the cross my own sinfulness reflected back at me I have not begun to know the meaning of sin. Sin progresses until it will stop at nothing: "I will ascend to the tops of the clouds, I will make myself like the Most High!" (Isaiah 14:14). Such conduct can end in nothing but self-destruction, and self-destruction is, in fact, the final product of sin. In raging against Jesus human nature raged in the effort to destroy its own best self. But it was no more effective against the ocean of God's mercy than a fist shaken at the stars.

Jesus allowed us to destroy his body to indict not us but our wickedness. By his death his grace works in us through the Holy Spirit to help us realize how badly sin infects us and how much we need him who is our redemption, our soundness, and our life.

God's tenderness, Christ's body lying on the rock of Calvary wounded from head to foot, is the indictment of wickedness. If I accept the indictment and beg for the healing his wounds can bring me, he will tenderly remind me that all these sufferings and cruelties he has endured are mine to offer in the Mass. Clothed in him I will be radiant with the shining robes of obedience that beg God to live in me and not to die there. It is a prayer that God must hear because of the loving obedience the human race has offered in the person of Jesus. What we have done to Jesus is an indictment of our sinfulness, but what the Jesus has endured for us is our perfect healing and final restoration to the paradise of God.

Prayer

O Lord my God, you who live everywhere, live always in my heart. With you living in me, my body and soul are a living heaven. Without you they are a desecrated temple. Have pity on me, O eternal, sovereign Lord God, and protect me from destroying your holy temple and my own immortal life in Jesus.

O Jesus, my Lord Incarnate, the cruelness of the sins that wounded you warn me of the evil of which my human nature is capable. But your lordly endurance reflects the noble obedience to God which this same nature we share can offer. Beloved Lord God, help me imitate not what we have done to you, but what you have done for us. Help me to realize that we obtain the good we desire not by sinning, but by refusing to sin. Every sin, every effort to play god, only makes us less like you, my God; but—almost beyond hope—every prayer and submission to your sovereignty makes us truly godlike. Thank you for assuring us of that. Thank you for the words of Saint Augustine: "God became man so that man might become God. The Lord of the angels became man today so that man could eat the bread of angels" (Christmas homily, Office, I, 541).

I yearn to eat daily the bread of angels so that I can share your very life, Jesus, and become more and more one with you and in you. I ask this with great confidence, my Jesus, for I know that you are the Vine and I the branch, and that you long to have the branches made like the Vine. Amen.

20

BLOOD OF JESUS

THE BODY OF JESUS hung upon the cross, dead. It was true death, for his soul had been severed from his body, and the body which Mary had borne now hung lifeless upon the cross in the late afternoon. Yet it was only one kind of death, bodily death. Jesus' human soul still lived on. It had descended to bring release to the prisoners who had so long waited for him to come and open the gates of heaven.

And Jesus the Word of God, in his divinity still lived everywhere as only God can live. Sole eternal Son, he inhabited celestial places and dwelt on in the bosom of the Father. Divine Son, now forever Incarnate, he was still united to his living human soul that was so joyously embraced by Abraham and Isaac and Jacob in their shattered prison. True God and true Man, his divinity watched over his dead body hanging on the cross. In three days he would reunite to that body his soul and from that moment his human life would go on forever.

The body of Jesus hung upon the cross, dead. Yet when the lance was raised and plunged into that breast no longer rising and falling with the sign of life, life flowed forth nonetheless. Blood and water flowed from his breast to give life and to purify, and it was from this life and purification that the Church was born. We, the living members of Christ, are the Church. It was we who were mystically born at that moment.

Life had long been identified with blood by the Jews. God said to them, "You shall not eat the blood of any creature, for the life of every creature is its blood; whoever eats it shall be cut off" (Leviticus 17:14b). When the Jewish priests offered sacrifice they could eat the flesh of the animals they slew but not drink the blood. They had to pour it out, had to give the blood back to God, Master of Life.

But unlike his brother priests, our Priest is himself the Master of Life. The human body which he took from Mary he offered in sacrifice, but unlike his brother priests among the Jews, this new Priest gives us the blood of his sacrifice to drink, for his sacrifice is our life: "Very truly I tell you, unless you eat of the flesh of the Son of Man and drink his blood, you have no life in you. Those who eat my flesh and drink my blood have eternal life, and I will raise them up the last day" (John 6:53–54).

Drinking the blood of Jesus brings about what it symbolizes: union with Jesus and sharing of his life. That is why the blood flowing from the wound piercing his Heart is the perfect symbol of his self-giving. "Let anyone who is thirsty," Jesus said, "come to me, and let the one who believes in me drink. As the scripture has said, 'Out of the believer's heart shall flow rivers of living water" (John 7:37–38). This living water from within Jesus is no less than the Holy Spirit, as John's Gospel tells us.

In Holy Communion the Christian responds to the invitation of Jesus. He drinks the blood of life from his wounded side by consuming his body and blood under the appearance of bread, and when possible by receiving his blood under the appearance of wine. For Jesus has come to be our life and our joy. He will make us find our inebriation in this union of divine love which only he was able to institute for it is beyond all human powers of self-giving.

Only the body of Jesus is heavenly bread. Only the blood of Jesus is the Wine which came down from heaven.

 ## Prayer of Saint Ignatius

Soul of Christ, sanctify me.

Body of Christ, save me.

Blood of Christ, inebriate me.

Water from the side of Christ, wash me.

Passion of Christ, strengthen me.

O good Jesus, hear me.

Within your wounds hide me.

Never suffer me to be separated from you.

From the evil enemy defend me.

At the hour of my death call me,

And bid me come to you,

That with your angels and Saints

I may praise you for ever and ever, Amen.

21

MOMENTS OF POSSESSION

A PERSON WHO HAS FALLEN deeply in love knows only one way to find happiness: possess the beloved! Though it be necessary to cross seas and move mountains, the lover must possess the loved one. And what if the Loved One be God himself? Then this driving need is intensified a hundred-fold. Men and women have struggled across spiritual deserts and wandered dark nights of the soul, finding no rest, no peace, no joy until they find the divine beloved. "Upon my bed at night I sought him whom my soul loves; I sought him, but found him not; I called him, but he gave no answer. 'I will rise now and go about the city, in the streets and in the squares; I will seek him whom my soul loves'" (Song of Solomon 3:1–2). To possess all else is nothing; to possess God is all.

To receive of the beloved's possessions is little, while to receive the beloved is everything because it includes all that belongs to the beloved. In the parable of the Prodigal Son the father assures his son that what he possesses is also his son's. And at the Last Supper Jesus said to his Father, "All mine are yours and yours are mine" (John 17:10). And Saint Paul wrote: "He who did not withhold his own Son, but gave him up for all of us, will he not with him also give us everything else?" (Romans 8:32). If the beloved gives himself he gives all, for who would surrender up his own person and then refuse a lesser gift? Who would treasure himself less than his possessions? To receive the beloved is to receive all he is and has and can obtain.

It is no mystery why the lover can't find joy until the beloved gives the gift of self, for joy is rest in the possession of our love. The ardent Christian cannot be satisfied apart from the perfect possession of God.

With longing Philip asked Jesus to show him God the Father and Jesus replied, "Whoever has seen me has seen the Father" (John 14:9). In Jesus we both see the Father and possess him, for through the possession of Jesus, God Incarnate, we gain possession of the whole Triune Godhead, Father, Son, and Holy Spirit. We can see this truth reflected in the Council of Florence's teaching that "These three persons are one God, not three gods; for the three persons have one substance, one essence, one nature, one divinity, one immensity, one eternity." Perfect joy is rest in the possession of God our love. Perfect possession of Jesus is perfect joy.

Longing is not yet possession, and how the true lover longs to possess the beloved! Longing is both joy and sorrow: joy because in hope the beloved is already possessed; sorrow because the possession is only in hope. What calamities might befall, and sweep away the beloved forever? What change might occur in the heart of the beloved? Might not one's own image fade from the attention of that heart and be lost from it forever?

With a certain anxiety, then, does the lover who is not yet possessor seek reassurances from the beloved. What if through one's own fault the beloved's affection should be forfeited? "Work out your salvation with fear and trembling," writes St. Paul to the Philippians (2:12). And Jesus himself warned: "Not everyone who says to me, 'Lord, Lord,' will enter the kingdom of heaven, but only the one who does the will of my Father in heaven" (Matthew 7:21). It is with good reason that Christian lovers, all too aware of their own inconstancy, long to enter into the eternal possession of their divine beloved.

It is proverbial that the lover is not satisfied with tender signs of love from the beloved, signs that everyone else can see. What great sign can the Christian unearth that signifies beyond doubt the self-giving of his divine beloved to him? By the very nature of love the lover needs such a great sign of reassurance, needs to know that "my beloved is to me, and I to him, whom my soul loves." To dare to hope for so great a sign from God seems like presumption, yet this is the daring of Christian love. And so good is God, the great beloved of humanity, that he manifests to the Christian the infallible, incontrovertible sign of his Self-giving. In Holy Communion God gives himself, Divinity, soul, body and blood to the one who receives him.

The true lover of God wants to be on fire with longing to receive daily this Eucharistic sign of God's self-giving, this sign which is not only sign but reality. Here is great happiness for here is possession. In this Communion that is holy the Christian lover finds hours of peace and joy and rest. "I found him whom my soul loves. I held him and would not let him go" (Song of Solomon 3:4).

Prayer

O Jesus, if you do not come to me this day, how much will I long for you! Jesus, I would choose your visit this day above the whole world and all its joys for all my days, for what is true joy to me but you?

Come then, Jesus, come to me in this great sign and reality of your self-giving. Bread with every good taste, nourish me daily so I won't faint with hunger along the way. Divine Shepherd, give me rest in green pastures, comfort me with your presence, let me rest a moment with you. Come daily, Jesus, and this strong Bread will carry me unflagging across the desert, and its delight will guide me unerringly to you. Amen.

22

FOUNTAIN OF LOVE

THERE IS LOVE that is a fountain of life and love that deals the kiss of death. Deep human love brings life to others or deepens the life already in them. But when we love too little we destroy the thing we love.

Cain loved his brother Abel, the dear companion of his youth. But he loved him too little and in the moment of crisis his jealousy overpowered his love. He killed his brother. We too can kill the things we love. All people love freedom, as we see today in the fierce worldwide struggle for political freedom. Yet many who love freedom kill their greatest freedom—spiritual freedom—by sinning. They become the slaves of sin.

Only too often man and wife kill one another's love by selfishness, meanness and bickering. The unsurpassed beauty of a love radiant on their wedding day becomes the depressing sight of a house divided and falling.

What is this mystery by which love can bring death? Small love brings death because under false pretense of being great it gains entrance to the inner sanctum of another's soul where all cruelness is terribly out of place and the smallest wound can slay because it strikes love down where love lives unprotected.

The love of man and wife bring them together in the act meant to intensify their love and their union and their exaltation and send their love forth as a sheer gift of life to another. Yet even here a love that is too small collapses before the selfishness that deliberately seeks to stifle the gift of life, or even to destroy what it has created.

God's love is never thus. God's love gives being and life. All that God made he loved. So great is his love for us that he gave us his Son, frail in human nature, to live among us. But because our love for Jesus was too small, we took his life.

Not like our love is Christ's. In the ritual renewal of the very act in which we took his life Jesus comes to give us everlasting life. Only in the mystery of Calvary renewed does bread become the body of Jesus and wine his blood. In these gifts of his love is our immortal life. His love is victor over our death.

Our potentially death-dealing loves can all become fountains of life for others if they are purified at the Fountain of Life. Our small love can become great love by frequent immersion of our hearts in the burning Heart of Jesus. He himself has given us the command to love greatly: "Just as I have loved you, you also should love one another." Jesus shares his life-giving love with us in Holy Communion. Not that Communion dispenses with our efforts. With Communion we can still fail unless we daily walk the way of love. But without Communion we can hardly succeed no matter how we try. Holy Communion can make our love the godlike love that gives life to others, or rouses to joy the slumbering life they have. Holy Communion can so charge our love with the grace of eternal life that our love can be a fountain inside of which bubbles the Fountain of the Life of all.

 ## Prayer

O Jesus, true Fountain of Life, let me always drink of this Fountain. I thirst for this spring of Life. Alongside these waters will I settle. Here will I dwell where I am cooled and refreshed and inebriated with love.

Drinking daily from the Eucharistic Fountain of your love, my Jesus, may I well over with the love that helps to bring the gift of spiritual life to others. May I become a stream which will lead others to its Source where they too may find rest and the Love that is their only true Life. Amen.

23

---— ≋ ——---

THREE LOVES OF CHRIST

WHEN ADAM'S BREAST first began to rise and fall with a life created directly by God himself, who could imagine what was in store? Who could have dreamed that the infinite God, the infinite pure Spirit, the almighty Creator, would so love his tiny creature that he would descend and wrap himself in the garments of that same frail human nature? Yet this unimaginable descent from the heights of divinity to the lowly depths of human soul and body was already then the purpose and plan of man's Creator. He knew from all eternity how terribly man would long for him as God and Savior, he who could understand such urgent love because it was only a pale reflection of his own.

By contemplating Adam, holy and good as he came from the hand of God, and lifting our eyes to the God who made him, we can gain some glimmer of the three loves of Jesus Christ for us. Jesus, last Adam, is both Man and God. To know his love for us we must understand the love of both. Through the Incarnation, his human Heart was given the noble task of representing not only the purest of sensible and spiritual human love, but even of symbolizing the uncreated divine Love itself.

Thus the physical Heart of the Man Jesus is like every human heart a center of sensible love, and a symbol of the love of the human soul; but it is above all a messenger from the Holy Trinity sent to tell by the tale of human love, the story of God's own love, which is really too great to be borne by anything outside of God himself.

The Heart of Jesus, then, is the symbol of the God-man's threefold love for us. First there is the sensible love of that Heart itself. We must often grieve and confess to God that we do not feel within our cold hearts the love for him that we long to have. With Jesus it is not so. His sinless soul and perfect sensibilities, perfectly faithful to God and the laws of human nature, never fail to express by feeling and emotion the same love that wells up within his human spirit at thought of all those he loves. He who prayed "with loud cries and tears" (Hebrews 5:7) felt within himself the whole tender symphony of human emotions and loves. He wept over the city he loved; he groaned and wept over a dead friend, and his friends' weak faith. In those hours of tender and loving fellowship the night before he died he made great new revelations and promised the threefold gift of God. For as though carried away by the surges of his own love that night he gave himself completely, humanity and divinity, together with his Father and his Spirit. And as though his love made him forget our wretchedness and meanness he commanded us in turn to "love one another as I have loved you." Who but Christ could have the confidence in human nature to command such a love? Yet Christ knew it was possible to us because he contained it in his own human heart.

Sensible love for us within the heart of Jesus stands as a clear symbol of the spiritual love for us within his soul. Spiritual human love is a true image of God's own love for it has the power to thrust beyond the confines of death and go on forever because the human soul is immortal. If it be deep love it can face death bravely because it can survive death. "No one has greater love than this, to lay down one's life for one's friend" (John 15:13).

These words of Jesus test our love and prove his. By his own love Jesus knew what true love is. This made him lonely for he could not be deceived by sentimental love that collapses under the burden love is asked to bear. "Do you also want to leave?" he asked his Apostles when many followers abandoned him because their love failed to sustain the eucharistic faith he asked. During the passion, Peter denied knowing Jesus. Jesus "turned and looked at Peter," and that strong man wept bitterly (Luke 22:61–62). No one who has known love has difficulty understanding those bitter tears. Peter's love was not the fearless love he thought it was. It was not strong as death; it was not even strong as the threat of death.

This betrayal by Peter did not destroy the love of Jesus for Peter. It was God's love for sinners that brought Christ. "In this is love, not that we loved God but that he loved us and sent his Son to be the atoning sacrifice for our sins" (1 John 4:10). This love of the human soul of Jesus is one of the glories of heaven where he stands now radiant with triumphant love, interceding for us.

The human heart of Jesus, vibrant with its own sensible love, and symbolic of the spiritual love of his human soul, is also symbolic of his third and greatest love, his uncreated divine love. For God did not cease being God when he took on the human nature of the men and women he had created. He did not cease to love divinely but rather he only lighted a new light of love in the breast of Christ which symbolizes the eternal love of the Son our Redeemer and of the Father our Creator and of the Holy Spirit our Sanctifier.

Even on earth we can gain some understanding of the love of the human heart and soul of Jesus. But only in heaven's experience of the torrents of the love of God will we know how little we comprehended the love of the Father, Son, and Holy Spirit.

 ## Prayer

What can inspire me more than your love, O Christ? What can give me hope of faithfully loving like your human example? Your love floods my soul with a great tenderness and a great longing to return love for love. Your selfless, fearless life lived in the human nature we have in common is always before my eyes. When you sought nothing but our good can I seek nothing but myself? Knowing that you actually longed for the sufferings that would redeem me, can I long for nothing but my own pleasures? You shared our flesh and blood, Jesus. Your pains were no less than our pains, your sufferings certainly not less than our sufferings. With your help and grace, Lord Jesus, I too can live the life of a child of God.

Make my spirit so pure and so like yours, Jesus, that my heart will catch the fire of my soul's love for you, and I will offer you a love after your own heart. Amen.

24

---— ≈ ———

TOUCHSTONE OF LOVE

GENUINE LOVE for Jesus is a priceless treasure. Sentimental love, on the other hand, is far worse than useless. It leads to the dangerous illusion that if the going gets tough it's okay to sin because "Jesus will understand."

Sentimental love makes this presumption because it thinks it has the privilege of true love. True love can count on everything, because by its nature it recoils from anything unfitting. That is why Saint Augustine could say, "Love God and do what you will." True love can no more do what is unfitting than a crystal fountain can spout polluted water. A fountain that brings forth polluted water is not a crystal fountain, nor is a love that habitually gives way to serious habitual sin as yet a true, strong love. Jesus said it plainly: "They who have my commandments and keep them are those who love me" (John 14:21). Our love is made visible in the actions it brings forth. By these it must be judged, as the tree is judged by its fruit.

There is no room for sentimental love in the teaching of Christ, as we can see by this norm for testing love which he gave us. Love is the source of actions faithful to Christ, and where this obedience is lacking love is lacking. This is the cornerstone of Christ's teaching on love.

Jesus repeated this truth in other ways. Recall his warning that "Not everyone who says to me, 'Lord, Lord,' will enter the kingdom of heaven, but only the one who does the will of my Father in heaven" (Matthew 7:21). In the parable of the ten foolish virgins, consider the words of the bridegroom to them: "I do not know you" (Matthew 25:12). The words make the mind reel. The bridegroom may refuse to have anything further to do with the foolish virgins but how can he deny knowing them in the past? Are we faced with a contradiction—or a change of identity brought about by sinful conduct? Involved here is the mystery of iniquity.

It is almost as if grave sin changes our identity, as baptism did. By baptism we were reborn in Christ. The character of that rebirth cannot be erased, but it can be layered over with corruption. It as though by sin we are configured to Satan. And in fact when certain unbelieving listeners made the claim, "Abraham is our father," Jesus retorted: "You are from your father the devil" (John 8:39, 44). Genuine love of God instinctively knows this and abhors sin. Sentimental love that presumes to sin gravely loses what identity it had with true love. It is no longer recognizable.

Genuine love knows Jesus is with us always to inspire us. He strengthens us to carry out God's will whatever the cost. Genuine love draws strength from the wounds of Jesus, wounds suffered in the service of love. Sentimental love presumes that the holiness of God's will can be degraded to the level of sin and even made to approve of sin. Sentimental love thinks it can make God come to want what it wants, though what it wants is sinful.

Genuine love knows that Jesus will always forgive sin repented, but he can never approve of sin. He cannot even live in peaceful coexistence with sin. Genuine love knows these truths because it knows Jesus. Sentimental love is ignorant of these truths because not only does not Jesus know it but it does not know Jesus.

 ## Prayer

O Jesus, love of you is the gift I beg from your heart. Your human Heart wounded for love of me, burning with love, is the pattern of love to which I consecrate myself.

My God, fill my heart with a passionate love for you that will move mountains and give all. Breathe into me a love worlds removed from sentimental love that gives nothing but sighs and does nothing but take. Let me sigh and long for you, O God, but let my love be more in action than in word.

Jesus, I give you all I have and am and can obtain. Take my heart and give me yours that I may always live in you and you in me. Amen.

25

THE LAST THINGS

A SOBER EUCHARISTIC SPIRITUALITY necessarily includes all the major teachings of Jesus. If the love of the Eucharistic Christ is deep, it is not only willing but eager to absorb all his teachings. It wants to rest on the bedrock of reality and not on illusion. Love of Jesus hopes to endure forever and to assure this hope it builds its nest on the eternal truths of God.

Genuine love of God is the source of a true filial fear of God—fear of displeasing him. But as Saint Ignatius taught, it is wise "to beg for a deep sense of the pain which the lost suffer, that if because of my faults I forget the love of the eternal Lord, at least the fear of these punishments will keep me from falling into sin." That is a good reason to take to heart Christ's teaching on the last state of man: heaven or hell.

One need not look far for the teaching of Christ on hell. Jesus warned of hell time and time again. In clear and terrible words Jesus warned of hell that would last forever: "If your right eye causes you to sin, tear it out and throw it away; it is better for you to lose one of your members than for your whole body to be thrown into hell" (Matthew 5:29).

Thus Jesus taught us to fear not so much God but sin and the Tempter and occasions of sin; or if God, God who because he is the just Judge of last appeal must see that unrepentant sinners find their fit place: "Do not fear those who kill the body but cannot kill the soul; rather fear him who can destroy both soul and body in hell" (Matthew 10:28).

Any spirituality that ignores this clarion warning of Christ is at best a fool's paradise. If Eucharistic spirituality with its great peace and fearless love seems to ignore the warning, it is only an appearance. The reality beyond the appearance is that this devotion generates a love which casts out fear because it casts out every intention of sinning.

This love that casts out fear is nourished on a vivid awareness, not so much of hell, but of heaven. The reason is that the Eucharist brings a man into direct contact with the last things, with Alpha and Omega, with God Incarnate, the slain and risen Lamb. How can one who is in daily contact with the Beginning and the End forget the last things? How can one help but think of heaven who daily communes with the Man who is in heaven? "For where your treasure is, there your heart will also be" (Matthew 6:21). Eucharistic spirituality does not ignore but rejoices in the last things, for the last of all is Jesus Christ in God.

Prayer

O Jesus, my treasure is where you are, my God and Savior. Be the Beginning and the End, the First and Last to me. I want you completely, O Lord Jesus. I accept you completely in all that you teach me of faith and morals. You are the Way and in traveling this way I abide in you. You are Truth and in receiving your truths I receive you. How can I shut my heart to anything you say if it means rejecting you whom I possess because I have believed?

Jesus, God of my heart, speak to me and teach me all you have revealed. I believe that everything you have taught leads only to you. Thoughts of eternal punishment turn me from evil and thoughts of you turn me to good. And in all things good I can find you their Creator. O Jesus let me not fear to meditate on any truths that you have revealed; or at least Jesus, give me the grace to embrace even the truths I fear, for I believe that I will soon discover that what I have embraced with fear is only you. Amen.

26

SELF–FULFILLMENT

SELF-GIVING IS THE LAW of self-fulfillment for all that exists from highest to lowest. And total self-surrender to Jesus in the Eucharist seems to be the highest self-fulfillment attainable here on earth.

Surrender of the earth to the strong arms of the sun's gravity makes her the sharer of the sun's life-giving effulgence. Were earth not the captive of the sun it would be a black and lonely hulk plunging through interstellar space, cold and dead.

Inert chemicals of lifeless soil surrender themselves to the secret powers of the growing plant and are invested with the mystery of life and the beauty of the lily of the valley. And then the honeyed center of the flower offers itself to the probing bee and is transformed into her sentient life and sees and tastes its former self.

The animals themselves, when they are eaten by *homo sapiens* and drawn up by anabolism into the highest corporal synthesis, can not only see and taste, but can even think about their former selves. Yet in all these wonderful metamorphoses there is a second, tragic law of nature at work: When absorbed into the higher form of life the lower form loses its identity. The fatted calf which supplies a human being's dinner becomes part of a human being but is no longer a calf.

The supernatural symbiosis brought about by eating the Bread of Life is not subject to this second, tragic law of nature, but only to that happy first law. We eat the body and blood of Christ—and in a way we become *his food!* For the ones who eat ordinarily change the food into themselves, but in the Eucharist we do not make Christ part of us. Christ makes us part of him, part of his Mystical Body. In becoming part of Christ, we do not cease to be ourselves. We enter into the life of the God–Man but do not cease to be persons.

We are not pantheists who teach that all things lose their individual identity in God. We are Christians who know that the infinite abyss between God and man is bridged only by Jesus, God-become-man, and that if we are to share in the life of God we can do so only by mystical union with the human nature of Jesus, for his human nature alone is personally united to the divine Son of God.

We gain this union with the humanity of Christ by baptism and Holy Communion. The Church teaches that Jesus' "body and blood are truly contained in the sacrament of the altar ... that, for the enacting of the mystery of unity, we may take from his substance as he himself took from our substance" (Fourth Lateran Council, Constitutions, 1). In this unimaginably sublime union we are taken up into the life of Jesus, but he does not destroy our identity when he absorbs us into himself any more than he destroyed the perfection of his human nature when he united it to his divine nature. Rather he perfects our identity through our union with him.

We Christians are truly ourselves only when we are the parts of Christ knowing and loving him. We are the "one Christ, loving himself," because in him alone what he takes into union with himself does not lose its identity but rather remains integral while also becoming part of him.

In Jesus we are many persons in a supernatural unity with and in one divine Person. More surely than the soil drawn up into the living lily of the valley, we are lifted up into a higher, more incomprehensible life. We share through the human nature of Jesus a created share in the pre-existent Life in Jesus that is eternal and divine.

The sacraments that graft us into the Vine do not bestow a self-fulfillment that consists solely in the gift of eternal life. "As though to breathe were life!" exclaims Tennyson's Ulysses in contempt. No, we human beings are intellectual creatures who long not merely for life, but for life shared with others. We seek fulfillment in communion with other human beings. But now, in the supernatural life which God has ordained for us, our fulfillment lies in eternal communion with the Lord God himself. The sweet joy of life together swells to an eternal torrent of pleasure when the fellowship is with God. "I have said these things to you," said Jesus at the first Communion banquet, "so that my joy may be in you, and that your joy may be complete" (John 15:11).

"Drink to me only with thine eyes," whispers the poet, mindful of the sweetness of spiritual communion. God the ineffably pure Spirit who knows the inexpressible longings of our hearts has opened for us a way to total union with him. He has set out for us a banquet where the wine is his blood and the food his flesh, a banquet which opens to us the supernatural world where the pitiful limits of human fellow-ship are no more and human hearts can expand into godlike torrents of joyful fulfillment. When the branches are intertwined with the Vine who became like them, they ascend upward with him to the heaven of heavens when they become like him. The Lord God walks once again with his creatures in the Garden of Pleasure. This time it is forever.

 ## Prayer

O Vine of heaven, I am an alien branch grafted into you. It is by faith that I live in hope and love of you. May the divine sap of your power flow into my soul and complete the transforming action you have begun, making me at last true stock at home in the house of God.

Long ago I was drawn to love the true, the good and the beautiful as it is personalized in you, my Lord and God. You so won my heart that there was no longer any room within it for selfish thoughts of fulfillment, but only for giving you my love until I had no more to give.

Then I began to understand your words that "[T]his is eternal life, that they may know you, the only true God, and Jesus Christ whom you have sent" (John 17:3). You created us in your triune likeness, my God, so that communing is our life.

You so form us by faith in your Eucharistic presence that if we cultivate love of your gift, we can spend time by the hour before you in the Blessed Sacrament, and we can commune with you in the

Eucharist daily and never weary of so loving and unearthly a mystery.

When Mother Church at last defined the truth of your Mother Mary's Immaculate Conception, she herself added yet another note to its mystery by appearing to Saint Bernadette and declaring, "I am the Immaculate Conception." If you, Jesus, should appear to me and say, "I am the Real Presence," could I not respond, "My Lord, you have already taught me that in so many ways. Is that not why you see so much of me before your tabernacles?"

O Real Presence, I await the eternal moment when my faith, that fountain of hope in you, will give way to the vision of you in all your glory. In that vision, you are the fountain of the love by which I will love you forever. When shall I see your face, O God of loveliness?

Scripture Index